HC 256.3 .A585 1983 146038
Aldcroft, Derek Howard
British economy between
 the wars

THE BRITISH ECONOMY BETWEEN THE WARS

Derek H Aldcroft

University of Leicester

Philip Allan

First published 1983 by

PHILIP ALLAN PUBLISHERS LIMITED
MARKET PLACE
DEDDINGTON
OXFORD
OX5 4SE

© Derek H Aldcroft 1983
All rights reserved

British Library Cataloguing in Publication Data

Aldcroft, Derek H.
The British economy between the wars.
1. Great Britain Economic conditions — 1918–1945.
I. Title
330.941'082   HC256

ISBN 0-86003-800-9
ISBN 0-86003-900-5 Pbk

Set by Midas Publishing Services Limited, Oxford
Printed at the Pitman Press, Bath

Contents

Preface v

Introduction 1

1 Growth of the Economy 4

2 Fluctuations in Economic Activity 12

3 Demographic Trends 21

4 The Structure of the Economy 29

5 Agriculture 36

6 Industrial Production 41

7 Industrial Structure and Business Organisation 51

8 Transport and Communications 58

9 The Distributive Trades 66

10 Overseas Trade 72

11 The Balance of Payments   **79**

12 Financial Institutions   **83**

13 Currency and Credit   **90**

14 Public Finance   **98**

15 Prices, Wages, Incomes and Employment   **107**

16 Social Policy and Material Welfare   **114**

17 Life and Leisure in a Two Nation World   **121**

18 Unemployment and Economic Policy   **133**

The Interwar Years in Retrospect   **144**

General Reading List   **146**

Index   **147**

Preface

This short volume provides an introductory survey to Britain's interwar economy. It covers all major aspects of the economy and each chapter has a set of study questions and a guide to further reading, with a general reading list at the end of the book. The book is suitable for introductory courses in universities and colleges, as well as for sixth form and adult education courses in the modern period.

DEREK H. ALDCROFT
University of Leicester, October 1982

Acknowledgement

The photographs used in this book are reproduced by kind permission of the BBC Hulton Picture Library, as also is the cover photograph, which depicts a traffic jam by the Royal Exchange and Bank of England in 1922.

Introduction

The interwar years have become one of the most controversial periods in British economic history. This has not always been the case. Not so many years ago it would probably have been regarded as heresy to suppose that there was anything good to say about the period, such was the distress caused by high unemployment, falling exports and collapsing basic industries. Yet when scholars got to work on compiling comprehensive aggregate data, it transpired that the traditional picture of the period required modification in several respects. Notwithstanding the difficulties of the period, it was nonetheless apparent that real incomes rose steadily, the newer industries, housebuilding and the service trades expanded significantly, and the rate of growth of the economy was quite respectable compared with past standards, while there were substantial gains in social welfare. Generally in these years the range of consumer options widened appreciably.

Thus the student of the period is presented with some striking contrasts which he finds difficult to reconcile when so many people were without work. If the economy was not performing too badly, why then were not more people able to find work? This paradox is not so difficult to resolve if one bears in mind that it was a period of significant structural transformation arising partly out of the changing economic relationships wrought by the war and partly out of the natural process of economic development. Economies like firms do not stand still; they are continually adapting and adjusting to changing market and technological conditions, and the strength of the transforming process will vary over time. The British case in the interwar period was perhaps more prominent than most (though Sweden had a comparable experience) simply because the shift to a new industrial and technological base was greater than in the case of many other countries. This was because Britain had devoted such a large proportion of resources to the key staple industries of the nineteenth century which went ex-growth for one reason or another soon after the end of the First World War. These industries, moreover, were severely overmanned and they were located mainly in the northern half of the country, while the newer and expanding sectors of the economy were to be found in the Midlands and the South. The growth sectors of the economy could not, in the short term, absorb the displaced labour of the old staples, partly because the scale of the fall-out was so large and sudden, and partly because of the mobility and training problems presented by the process of structural adaptation.

The unemployment problem of the period assumes wider significance given the inability or reluctance of governments to do very much about it. However, as we shall see, it is doubtful whether there was both a quick and viable solution to the problem, since any attempt to generate employment rapidly would have run up against financial constraints and impaired the long-term viability of the economy.

This volume for the most part does not seek to raise the level of controversy. Indeed, it is designed rather with the opposite in mind, namely that of providing a short unbiassed survey of the developments in the economy as a whole and the main sectors and institutions of the economy. It does stress the importance of the structural

INTRODUCTION

issue however, and in the last chapter an element of controversy is introduced in the discussion of policy options with regard to the unemployment issue.

1 Growth of the Economy

Despite frequent fluctuations and heavy unemployment during the interwar years, the British economy was far from being stagnant in this period. It is true that had resources been more fully utilised the growth performance of the economy might have been better, and certainly the absolute volume of output would have been greater. Throughout the period there was rarely less than one million unemployed or about 10 per cent of the insured workforce, while many of the older staple industries operated far below full capacity. Nevertheless, considerable expansion did take place, especially in the newer sectors of the economy, and by the end of the period income and production levels were a good deal higher than those of 1913.

The war of 1914–18 checked the growth of the British economy. Although sectors supplying the products for the war machine expanded, those producing civilian goods contracted and the net effect was a check to expansion. Probably some five to six years' annual growth was lost, since it was not until 1920 that incomes and production approached prewar levels. At the end of the war real income per head (or income per capita) was very similar to that of 1913, though the tentative nature of some of the statistics for this period makes exact specification impossible. The sharp slump following the boom of 1919-20 meant that the economy grew little in the early 1920s, so that it was not until well into the 1920s that levels of activity exceeded the prewar base. Thereafter progress was steady if unspectacular through to 1929. Table 1 provides comparative growth rates of several economic indicators over a range of years. Some of the data need to be treated with caution since estimates for earlier years are at best tentative, while several revisions have been made in recent years.

It can be seen that for the decade of the 1920s the rates of growth of total output, industrial production and consumers' expenditure were very similar to the long-term averages over the period 1870-1913, though somewhat higher than in the decade or so prior to the war (1900-13). In fact, perhaps one of the main features of Britain's growth is the remarkable degree of stability between periods, 'almost as if the range of 2 to 2½ per cent per annum had been meted out to the British economy by divine grace — or, in the eyes of many critics, by divine retribution' (von Tunzelmann in Floud and McCloskey (1981)). The impact of the war can be seen by examining the period 1913-29 when rates of growth were abnormally low. An additional factor in this period was the sharp contraction in exports which can be attributed largely to the collapse of export markets of the basic industries. The one brighter spot was the relatively strong growth in productivity arising partly from the severe shake-out of labour from the older industries after 1920.

The economic crises of 1929-32 imposed a further check to long-term growth, though income and consumption held up remarkably well in Britain compared with many other countries. Recovery, moreover, set in fairly early and it was sustained by the sharp rise in consumption compared with the 1920s, so that by the end of the 1930s most indices had far surpassed their previous peaks in 1929. Thus over the years 1929-38 growth rates were fairly

Table 1 Average Rates of Growth of Selected Economic Indicators in the UK (per cent per annum)

	(1)	(2)	(3)	(4)	(5)	(6)	(7)
1870–1913	1.9	1.0	1.1	2.1	0.6	2.7	0.8
1870–1938	1.6	0.9	1.2	2.1	–	0.8	0.8
1900–13	1.5	0.9	0.9	1.7	0.2	4.2	0.6
1913–29	0.5	0.5	1.5	1.4	–	−1.3	0.4
1913–38	1.0	0.8	1.3	1.9	–	−2.3	0.7
1920–29	1.9	1.3	–	2.8	3.8	1.6	0.7
1920–38	1.9	1.4	–	2.8	2.8	−1.2	1.0
1929–38	1.9	1.4	0.9	2.7	1.8	−4.0	1.4
1950–60	2.7	2.3	2.3	3.0	2.2	1.8	2.1

Column (1) Gross Domestic Product (GDP)
      (2) GDP per capita
      (3) GDP per man-hour
      (4) Industrial production (including building)
      (5) Industrial productivity
      (6) Exports
      (7) Consumers' expenditure per capita

Sources:

Cols. 1, 2, 4, and 7 C.H. Feinstein, *National Income, Expenditure and Output of the United Kingdom, 1855–1965* (Cambridge, 1972)

Col. 3 A. Maddison, 'Long Run Dynamics of Productivity Growth', *Banca Nazionale del Lavoro Quarterly Review*, 128 (March 1979)

Col. 5 E.H. Phelps Brown and S.J. Handfield-Jones, 'The Climacteric of the 1890s: A Study in the Expanding Economy'. *Oxford Economic Papers*, 4 (1952) and London and Cambridge Economic Service, *Key Statistics of the British Economy 1900–1966*

Col. 6 A.H. Imlah, *Economic Elements in the Pax Britannica* (Cambridge Mass., 1958) and *Key Statistics* similar to those recorded in the 1920s and again somewhat better than before 1914. The main black spot was exports which fell by 4.0 per cent per annum as against a rise of similar magnitude before the war.

Taking the interwar period as a whole (1920–38), we find that rates of growth of total output and consumers' expenditure were very similar to the long-term averages before 1914, but that industrial production and productivity grew somewhat faster. Exports, however, contracted by 1.2 per cent per annum, whereas before 1914 they registered strong growth. Compared with the decade or so before 1914 growth generally was more buoyant in the interwar years, particularly in industrial production and productivity. During the later nineteenth century and through to 1914 there was some slowing down in the rate of economic progress, though recent research indicates that it was not as marked as originally thought. By contrast the interwar period seems to have experienced some acceleration in growth, even if of modest dimensions. Certainly most indices of activity register quite respectable rates of growth and the poor export performance provides the only major exception to this general conclusion. Furthermore, given the difficult international economic climate of this period, interwar growth performance compares reasonably well with that of other periods listed in Table 1.

The Second World War brought a further check to overall expansion, though some sectors of the economy, such as chemicals and metals, experienced substantial growth in output. By the end of the war total output and industrial production were no greater than they had been in 1938. There was probably some small increase in real income per head throughout the war period, though much of the gain accrued to the wage earning class whose earnings rose more rapidly than the cost of living.

How did Britain's performance compare with that of other countries? Here the problems of analysis are somewhat greater because of the limited amount of reliable data for cross-country comparisons. While there are continuous series of domestic output and industrial production for several countries, the estimates are continually being revised, so making reliable comparison hazardous. There are, moreover, few satisfactory estimates for the year 1920. As it happens this is not really a serious drawback, since 1920 is not a particularly suitable year for international comparisons. This is because Britain's recovery from the war effort was fairly rapid, so that by 1920 her output levels were similar to those in 1913, though in the following year they fell away sharply. On the other hand, some European countries took much longer to regain the prewar base, while in other cases distortions were caused by rapid inflation. Thus in many respects 1920 is an unsuitable benchmark year and a fairer comparison can be gained by using 1913 as a base. Such a choice as benchmark also has the additional advantage in that it provides a reasonable indication of the gains and losses wrought by war.

In Table 2 rates of growth of domestic output and output per man-hour are given for several countries including Britain. In the period up to 1929 Britain lagged behind most other countries. This can be attributed primarily to the weaker nature of the boom of the later 1920s in this country compared with abroad. However, during the following decade the position was reversed. Most countries suffered more severely than Britain in the slump of 1929–32, while in many cases the recovery was slow and protracted. This was especially the case in France, Belgium, Canada and the United States, all of which failed to regain or surpass their 1929 levels of activity. By contrast, Britain's recovery from the depression was quite vigorous and only four countries, Germany, Norway, Denmark and Sweden, recorded a better performance in total output over the years 1929–38. In fact, this is probably the only period in modern times when Britain has secured a place near the top of the growth league table. The better showing in the 1930s partly compensated for the poor track record in the previous decade, though for the entire period 1913–38 Britain's comparative performance was scarcely spectacular as a glance at Table 2 will show.

As might be expected, Britain's relative importance in the world economy declined in the interwar years, especially in the first half of the period. This was, of

Table 2 Average Rates of Growth of Gross Domestic Product and Output per Man-Hour (per cent per annum)

	1913–38 GDP	1913–38 GDP per man-hour	1913–29 GDP	1913–29 GDP per man-hour	1929–38 GDP	1929–38 GDP per man-hour
Belgium	0.9	1.5	1.4	1.8	0.0	1.0
Denmark	1.9	1.8	1.9	2.6	2.1	0.4
France	0.8	2.5	1.4	2.3	–0.4	2.7
Germany	2.1	1.7	1.2	1.4	3.8	2.4
Italy	1.6	2.3	1.6	2.0	1.5	3.0
Netherlands	2.2	1.5	3.2	2.4	0.3	–0.1
Norway	3.0	2.8	2.9	2.8	3.0	2.6
Sweden	2.7	2.4	2.8	2.4	2.3	2.4
Switzerland	2.0	2.4	2.8	3.2	0.6	1.0
Canada	1.5	0.8	2.4	1.3	–0.2	–0.1
USA	1.7	2.2	3.1	2.3	–0.7	1.9
UK	1.1	1.3	0.7	1.5	1.9	0.9

Sources: Calculated from A. Maddison, 'Phases of Capitalist Development', *Banca Nazionale del Lavoro Quarterly Review,* 121 (June 1977) and 'Long Run Dynamics of Productivity Growth', *Ibid.,* 128 (March 1979)

course, nothing new; it merely represented the continuation of a trend which had set in well before the end of the nineteenth century. By 1913 Britain had lost her former predominant position in manufacturing production to the United States and Germany, though she still remained the world's largest exporter. In that year her share of the world manufacturing production was 14.0 per cent, compared with nearly 36 per cent for America and 15.7 per cent for Germany. By the end of the 1930s Britain's share had fallen to nearly 9 per cent, while the United States, Russia and Germany, in that order, were the three largest producers. The check to exports after the war resulted in a similar fall in Britain's share of world exports, though she managed to maintain her position as the world's leading trader of manufactured goods for most of the period. This loss of shares was only to be expected as other nations, especially some of the lesser developed countries such as Japan, increased the pace of their development. On the other hand, the sharp drop in Britain's standing before 1929 can be attributed partly to the fact that the boom of the later 1920s was less vigorous in this country than abroad. Conversely, in the 1930s, when Britain's economic performance improved relative to that of other countries, her relative position in the distribution of world manufacturing production and exports remained fairly stable. The aggregate relative decline can be seen from the data in Table 3.

Table 3 Gross Domestic Product per Head at US 1970 Prices ($)

	1870	1913	1929	1950
UK	956	1468	1582	2061
Average for 16 major developed countries	666	1205	1460	1836
UK as % of average	143.5	121.8	108.4	112.3

Source: A. Maddison, 'Phases of Capitalist Development', *Banca Nazionale Del Lavoro Quarterly Review*, 121 (1977).

Despite the relative decline in economic power one can scarcely describe the British economy as being in a state of complete stagnation during the interwar period. Growth might easily have been more rapid had all resources been fully utilised, but the achievements were by no means negligible. Industrial production rose by 62 per cent and real income per head by over 30 per cent between 1920 and 1938, and the rates of growth of most major indices were respectable, if not spectacular. But perhaps the most notable feature of the period is not that growth took place amidst heavy unemployment, but the fact that it was so unevenly distributed over time, between regions and between different sectors of the economy. Fluctuations in economic activity were quite frequent and often severe, the northern regions of the country were much less prosperous than their counterparts in the south, while some industries expanded rapidly as others declined. These differences reflected the structural transformation which was taking place in the British economy as it shifted away from heavy dependence on the old nineteenth century staples of coal, textiles, shipbuilding and the like.

Study Questions on Growth of the Economy

(a) Compare and contrast the performance of the British economy in the 1920s and 1930s.

(b) How did Britain's interwar growth compare with that of other countries?

(c) Why and to what extent did Britain decline in relative economic importancee after the First World War?

Recommended Reading on Growth of the Economy

Aldcroft, D.H., 'Economic Growth in Britain in the Inter-war Years: A Reassessment', *Economic History Review*, 20 (1967)

Alford, B.W.E., *Depression and Recovery? British Economic Growth 1918–1939* (London, 1972)

Von Tunzelmann, N., 'Britain 1900–45: a survey' in R. Floud and D. McCloskey (eds), *The Economic History of Britain since 1700*, Vol. 2, *1860 to the 1970s* (Cambridge, 1981)

Williams, L.J., *Britain and the World Economy, 1919–1970* (London, 1971)

2 Fluctuations in Economic Activity

The war of 1914–18 demanded many sacrifices. Resources were channelled into wartime needs and eventually, after some early improvisations, most forms of activity were rigorously controlled by the government. In the process many former markets for British exports were lost for ever, while a certain proportion of the country's overseas assets had to be liquidated. Despite control, wages and prices rose rapidly and by the end of the war they were more than twice the levels of 1914. Investment and replacement were delayed, which meant that capacity was strained to the limit in meeting wartime requirements. Despite great activity however, real incomes by the end of the war had changed very little, while on a per capita basis there had been a slight decline.

At the end of the war there was a large pent-up demand for basic necessities both at home and abroad and a considerable backlog of unspent purchasing power. Furthermore, the need for new investment was acute as a result of the lag in investment during hostilities. Thus after a short postwar downturn the economy picked up rapidly and by the summer of 1919 Britain was experiencing a boom of unprecedented proportions. The sharp upswing was encouraged by the abolition of many wartime controls in the first six months after the war, by lax monetary and fiscal policies and by the strong demand for exports. However, it was very much a price boom rather than one of production. Wages and prices rose rapidly, and speculation was rife, but total output barely regained the prewar level. Second-hand assets changed hands at vastly inflated prices. Most countries went through a similar experience during 1919–20.

The boom lasted approximately a year until the early spring of 1920, after which the collapse was even more dramatic than the original upswing. The origins of the downturn in the case of Britain may be traced to a falling off in consumer spending in the early months of 1920. This was accompanied by tighter monetary and fiscal policies especially in the spring of 1920 though, unlike the case of America, monetary restraint was not the initial cause of the breaking of the boom. In addition, the demand for British exports fell off sharply in the latter part of 1920 as economic conditions deteriorated abroad. By then economic activity was already falling rapidly and in the following year Britain was experiencing one of the worst depressions in history. Apart from investment, which was bolstered up by a large programme of subsidised housebuilding, all indices of activity fell sharply: industrial production by 18.6 per cent, exports by 30.1 per cent, total output by 12.1 per cent, real income by 3.2 per cent, employment by 14.4 per cent and wholesale prices by over one third. Unemployment rose to around 22 per cent of the insured workforce and the position was aggravated by strikes in many industries.

Though the unemployment position improved in the latter half of 1921, it was not until the beginning of the following year that production and output began to revive. In part the government's continued restraint in monetary and fiscal policy helped to delay the recovery. However, in 1922 production rose strongly and for the most part the recovery continued through to 1925. The initial upswing was generated by a revival in exports and

A queue of unemployed waiting outside a labour exchange in the 1920s. Unemployment was an acute and persistent problem of the interwar period, when there were rarely less than 1 million unemployed, or 10% of the insured workforce.

FLUCTUATIONS IN ECONOMIC ACTIVITY

by developments in the consumer goods industries, supplemented by growth in the newer industries and later by an upturn in building. An upsurge in investment did not take place until 1924 and 1925, but in terms of unemployment the recovery was by no means complete. Even at its lowest in June 1924, the number of unemployed was still around one million or 9.2 per cent of the insured population and it tended to rise thereafter. Nevertheless, the strength of the recovery was quite marked, so that by the mid-1920s income and production levels were above those of 1920 and 1913.

Expansion came to a temporary halt in 1926. This can be explained readily in terms of the industrial troubles of that year, notably the General Strike and the prolonged stoppage in coalmining. In comparison with 1921 the downturn was relatively mild and the main burden was borne by the heavy trades which were again affected by export losses. Some industries, such as vehicle manufacturing, building materials and electricity, continued to expand throughout 1926. Thus had it not been for industrial difficulties, it is very likely that economic activity would have continued on an upward trend during 1926. Subsequently the strength of the recovery was very much weakened. Compared with America and some European countries, Britain experienced a rather feeble boom in the later 1920s. Output increased more slowly than in the first half of the decade, while between 1927 and 1928 industrial production and investment fell. The dip in production was very modest however, being confined to one or two sectors such as building, iron and steel, and shipbuilding.

Several factors were responsible for the dampened nature of the boom of the later 1920s. The stock explanation is that exports were at the root of the trouble, their growth being constrained by high and inflexible wage costs and an overvalued currency. Furthermore, many of Britain's exports consisted of staple products, the demand for which was either declining or rising very slowly, while the recovery of European production together with the development of manufacturing in other countries curtailed the outlet for British products. However, too much emphasis must not be put on the export thesis. The volume of exports rose more rapidly than the industrial production between 1926 and 1929, though the prewar levels were not regained. The impact exerted by building and the newer growth industries, such as motor manufacturing, chemicals and electrical engineering, was much less marked than in the case of America. Building for example collapsed in 1927–28 and over the years 1926–29 there was a negative growth rate in construction. Most of the service industries, including transport and distribution, recorded only modest rates of expansion, while the rate of growth of some of the newer industries was no greater than the average for all industry and considerably lower than in the first half of the 1920s.

Whatever the causes of the weak boom in Britain there is no doubt that it helped to soften the impact of the subsequent depression. The economy did not overshoot itself leaving exhausted sectors in its wake as in America, so that the chances of early recovery were greater than in the latter case. It is generally assumed that the downturn itself originated in the United States and was transmitted to other countries via foreign trade. But in the case of Britain there is some doubt whether the initial impulse actually came from this direction. There could well have been a recession in Britain irrespective of what was happening in America. The crucial factor was Britain's export vulnerability, and in particular her heavy dependence on primary producing markets. The incomes of primary producers began to fall in the late 1920s and the turning point in the demand for British exports from South America, British India, the British Colonies, the Far East and South Africa, which absorbed some 40 per cent of British exports, occurred in the latter half of 1928. This naturally exerted a deflationary impact on the British economy. Thus signs of impending recession were already evident some six to nine months before the collapse of the American economy, which began in the summer of 1929.

The subsequent American crash greatly aggravated and accelerated deflationary tendencies in Britain. Since America was such an important element in the world economy, other countries were soon affected by the repercussions of the American downturn. American import demand declined and the flow of capital from that country was curtailed. This created severe problems for most countries, particularly debtor countries and primary producers, resulting in severe balance of payments problems which eventually culminated in the international liquidity crisis of 1931. Given the widespread ramifications of the American economy, coupled with the instability and weak financial position of many countries in the 1920s, it was almost inevitable that a slump of international dimensions and unparalleled severity would occur in the early 1930s.

In comparison with the experience of most other countries the depression in Britain was mild. The United States, for example, suffered declines of 37, 36, and 31 per cent in real income, industrial production and employment respectively, whereas the corresponding figures for Britain were 0.8, 11 and 4.7 per cent. Only in two respects, namely the decline in wholesale prices and the percentage unemployment at the bottom of the depression, did Britain fare as badly as the United States. In the third quarter of 1932 the number of unemployed rose to nearly three million of 22.7 per cent of the insured workforce. The volume of exports fell by well over a third. But the declines in real income and consumers' expenditure were quite modest and for the most part the depression was less severe than that of 1921.

Just as the weakness of the boom in the later 1920s helped to insulate the economy from the full impact of the slump, so the relative mildness of the downturn helped to ease the way for an early and vigorous recovery. Business confidence was not completely shattered in Britain as was the case in America and Germany, nor did the banking and financial system experience any serious strain, and any loss of confidence was partly restored by the government measures of 1931–32, including abandonment of gold and depreciation of the currency, the imposition of tariff protection, conversion to cheap money, and action designed to curtail public expenditure and balance the budget. Moreover, there was no lack of investment opportunities for business once revival began. Investment outlets had not been exhausted in the previous decade as they had been in America. The belated development of the newer industries and the shortage of housing in particular meant that there was plenty of scope for vigorous growth in the 1930s, despite the drying up of investment opportunities in the basic export-orientated industries. A further factor of some importance was the very high floor to income and consumption at the bottom of the depression. In fact consumption fell only in the final year and over the course of the downswing it actually rose. It was maintained principally by three factors: a substantial increase in the real incomes of wage earners largely as a result of improvement in the terms of trade, a shift in the distribution of income in favour of wage earning groups, and an overall increase in the average propensity to consume.

Though the main force of the depression had been spent by the end of 1931, it was not until the last quarter of 1932 that economic activity definitely began to improve. During the following year most economic indices rose and there can be little doubt that 1933 was the first full year of recovery. Though there were some signs of revival in export-sensitive industries after the devaluation in 1931, the real thrust to recovery came from the non-export sectors such as building and related activities, transport, electricity, and the newer manufacturing trades such as vehicles and certain service trades. By 1934 sustained growth had extended to most sectors of the economy, though it tended to be most vigorous in the new and domestically-based industries and least prominent in the old staples. Nevertheless, exports picked up smartly in 1934–35 which helped to revive the older industries. Investment also increased sharply in 1934, though recovery in employment was more modest and by the end of that year there were still over two million persons out-of-work or nearly 16 per cent of the insured workforce.

During the course of the next three years the pace of recovery continued practically unchecked. Virtually all industries expanded though the boom was primarily a domestic one, the leading sectors being construction, transport (especially road transport), the new industries (vehicles, electrical, manufacturing, etc.) and certain capital goods industries. Exports continued to increase, though they remained well below the pre-depression level even by 1937. The progress of recovery in these years was assisted by the revival of the world economy and the beginnings of rearmament.

By 1937 the record of achievement was considerable. Since 1932 real income had increased by 19 per cent, domestic output by over 25 per cent, industrial production by nearly 46 per cent, gross investment by 47 per cent and even exports by 28.4 per cent. Moreover, in absolute terms the level of economic activity was far higher than it had been in the peak years of 1929 and 1913. In fact these years witnessed the largest and most sustained period of growth in the whole of the interwar period and Britain's performance was better than that of most other countries. Yet despite the considerable increase in activity employment rose by less than 17 per cent, which suggests that recovery was accompanied by a considerable increase in productivity. Hence unemployment did not fall as far as might be expected and at the peak of the boom (third quarter of 1937) 1.4 million people were still without work (9.1 per cent of the insured labour force). However, the greater part of this consisted of structural unemployment, since most of the cyclical unemployment had been eliminated by this date.

By the middle of 1937 there were signs that the boom was coming to an end. The rate of growth of income and production slowed down during the course of the year and there were indications of a temporary drying up of investment opportunities. There was also a sharp downturn in exports in 1937–38. The recession however was relatively mild and short-lived. Industrial production and domestic output declined by one or two per cent, while real incomes and consumption continued to increase. Few industries suffered a sharp contraction in activity except for those dependent on exports such as shipbuilding, textiles and ferrous metals. By the beginning of 1939 the economy had resumed its upward trend and was backed by rearmament and later war.

Study Questions on Fluctuations in Economic Activity

(a) Why were fluctuations so intense during the interwar years?
(b) Examine the causes of the Great Depression of 1929–32.
(c) Why was the recovery in the 1930s so strong?

Recommended Reading on Fluctuations in Economic Activity

Aldcroft, D.H. and Fearon, P. (eds), *British Economic Fluctuations 1790–1939* (London, 1972)

Richardson, H.W., 'The Economic Significance of the Great Depression in Britain', *Journal of Contemporary History*, 4 (1969)

3 Demographic Trends

The First World War marked a turning point in the history of British, as well as European, population developments. Wartime casualties together with shifts in fertility and mortality rates led to a reduction in the rate of population growth. UK military deaths amounted to nearly three quarters of a million or just over 1.7 per cent of the 1914 population. The overall impact was greater than these figures imply, since most of the persons concerned were in the prime of life and constituted the most productive part of the labour force. Moreover, the population losses due to war are much larger than the figures for military deaths alone, since account has to be taken of civilian casualties arising from disease, famine and privation as well as military conflict, on the assumption that these would not have occurred had there been no war, together with the wartime deficit in the number of births. For the UK the first of these gave rise to a loss of over 300,000 persons, while the shortfall of births due to the war amounted to over 700,000. Adding together the estimated losses under the three headings gives a combined population deficit as a result of the war of just under 1.8 million, equivalent to

4.16 per cent of the 1914 population.[1] Although this was a lower rate of loss than for most other European countries, the net effect was that Britain's population remained stationary throughout the years 1914–19.

After the interruption of war, a steady rate of increase in population was maintained throughout the interwar period, though the rate was much slower than it had been in the nineteenth and early twentieth centuries. It can be seen from Table 4 that the British population increased fairly slowly between 1914 and 1945, compared to the doubling of population between 1851 and 1911.

The actual increase in population is a measure taking account of natural increase, that is the excess of births over deaths, and net migration. Table 5 shows these statistics for the period 1911–41 (the years in which censuses were taken are used here).

The number of births depends almost wholly on the number of married couples and the rate at which they

Table 4 Population Growth in Great Britain, 1914–45

Date	Population (000s)
1914	41,714
1918	38,836[a]
1921	42,770
1933	45,262
1939	46,465
1945	49,280

(a) Civilians only

Source: B.R. Mitchell and P. Deane, *Abstract of British Historical Statistics* (Cambridge, 1962), p. 10

---

1. The figures take no account of those disabled or injured by the war. For the basis of calculation see F.W. Notestein *et al.*, *The Future Population of Europe and the Soviet Union* (Geneva, 1944), p. 75.

Table 5 Births, Deaths and Migration in Great Britain, 1911–41 (000s)

Period	Births	Deaths	Natural Increase	Net Migration	Actual Increase
1911–21	9,466	6,670	2,796	−858	1,938
1921–31	7,935	5,344	2,591	−565	2,026
1931–41	6,930	5,770	1,160	+650	1,810

Source: *Report of the Royal Commission on Population*, Cmd. 7695 (HMSO, 1949)

have children, that is, the size of the family. The latter is seen as the key influence on the fall in the birth-rate. Birth control became a more widespread practice. The average family size fell from 4.35 in 1911 to 3.59 in 1939. The probable reasons for this overall decline are as follows:

(a) the declining number of infant deaths reduced the incentive to bring a large number of children into the world;
(b) leisure activities became increasingly important and so the economic and material inducements to family limitation continued;
(c) more importance was placed on a better quality of life for children, for example, a high standard of education — the less the number of children, the higher the outlay per child, the better the standard of education;
(d) the status of women had been, since 1914, greatly improving and this meant that more women were going out to work; and
(e) economic depression and bad times caused people to be less eager to have children.

During World War II the situation remained much the same and it was only towards the end of and after the war that the birth-rate increased.

The declining rate of population growth, which was chiefly a result of a fall in birth-rate, would have been much greater had there not been a substantial and significant fall in the death-rate. From the early twentieth century through to World War II the life table changed considerably. The number of infant mortalities was greatly reduced (after 1940 it began approaching a minimum level), and life expectancy was much longer. The reasons for this decline in mortalities include the following:

(a) advances and improvements in medicine;
(b) improved standard of living resulting in better diets; and
(c) health and hygiene improvements.

The only outstanding mortality figures were due to war losses, but apart from these the death-rate steadily decreased.

A very noticeable phenomenon in Britain was the 'ageing' or change in age distribution of the population. In 1911 those under 45 numbered 32,125,000 and those above that age, 8,705,000; by 1937 the respective totals were 31,836,000 and 14,377,000 — a 65 per cent increase in the latter category. As the figures in Table 6 show, there was a significant increase in life expectancy from the early twentieth century.

In the period 1914–30 a high net outflow of migrants was maintained. After 1931 the balance swung the other way — world-wide depression closed the doors to migrants

Table 6 Expectation of Life at Birth in England and Wales, 1910–38

Year	Male	Female
1910–12	52	55
1920–22	56	60
1930–32	59	63
1938	61	66

Source: W. Johnson, J. Whyman and G. Wykes, *A Short Economic and Social History of Twentieth Century Britain* (London, 1968), p. 23

from England and even compelled British expatriates to return to Britain. Added to this was an influx of political refugees from Europe. World War II did confuse the pattern, but on the whole the flow of immigrants continued in the 1940s (see Table 7).

During the interwar years there were two distinct geographical shifts in population both of which reversed the dominant trends of the nineteenth century. First, there was a marked shift in population away from the town centres towards the suburbs and second, there was a strong tendency for the South to gain population at the expense of the North.

The movement of population from the city centre to the outskirts was the most prominent feature in the distribution of population. For example, of the 131 districts of England and Wales which increased their population by 30 per cent or more between 1921 and 1931, no less than 116 were suburban areas, the remainder being seaside resorts. All the major urban areas experienced this centrifugal movement, with population at the centre remaining constant or even declining. Thus the central zones of the seven largest urban areas[2] showed a decline in population of 2.5 per cent between 1921 and 1938, whereas population in their suburban areas rose by 32 per cent. Between 1921 and 1938, three quarters of Britain's population growth (3.44 million) accrued to the suburbs of the 27 major conurbations.

This suburban migration was caused by a complex set of interdependent factors. People were encouraged to move to the suburbs because of increasing congestion and the unpleasant surroundings in city centres. At the same time, rising real incomes, improved suburban transport facilities and cheaper accommodation on the outskirts made the movement possible.

The causes of the inter-regional migration were not so complex, being determined largely by the absence or availability of jobs. The pattern of regional migration was that the depressed areas lost, and the prosperous areas

---

2. London, Manchester, Birmingham, Glasgow, West Yorkshire, Merseyside and Tyneside.

Typical suburban housing of the 1930s. Suburban migration was a notable feature of the interwar years, when over 4 million new houses were built.

gained, population. The balance of regional gains and losses through inter-regional migration is shown in Table 7.

The chief gains were made by London, the South-east and the South-west — a total of 1.1 million between 1923 and 1936, while the major losses were experienced by Wales, Scotland and north-east England — altogether a loss of just over 1.2 million. The worst affected region was Wales, where the population fell from 2,656,000 to 2,465,000 between 1921 and 1939. During the 1920s overseas migration provided some relief for redundant workers of the depressed regions, but in the following decade this tradional safety-valve was closed and a net inward movement of population occurred (Table 7).

That the southern regions gained considerably from regional migration was undoubtedly an important factor in the uneven distribution of the population increase between the wars. The overall population increase between 1921 and 1937 was 7½ per cent, while the figure for London, the South-east and South-west was 18 per cent,

Table 7 Average Annual Gains (+) or Losses (−) through Migration, 1923–36

	1923–31	1933–36
London and Home Counties	+62,205	+71,623
South-east	+8,733	+18,334
South-west	+10,582	+11,445
Midlands	−4,964	+5,521
North-west	−19,275	−6,942
North-east	−30,516	−24,180
Scotland	−37,559	+1,299
Wales	−31,350	−22,092
Net inward (+) or outward (−) balance of overseas migration	−42,144	+55,008

Source: M.P. Fogarty, *Prospects of the Industrial Areas of Great Britain* (London, 1954), p. 4

and for the Midlands it was around 11 per cent. All other areas expanded by less than the national average and Wales and the North-east lost absolutely. The South-east segment of the country accounted for roughly one third of the population of England and Wales in 1921, yet absorbed just over two thirds of the increase in population.

Study Questions on Demographic Trends

(a) Why did population growth slow down in the interwar years?
(b) What were the main changes in the distribution of population?
(c) What factors influenced migration in this period?

Recommended Reading on Demographic Trends

Fogerty, M.P., *Prospects of the Industrial Areas of Great Britain* (London, 1945)
Hubback, E.V., *The Population of Britain* (London, 1947)
Winter, J.M., 'Some Aspects of the Demographic Consequences of the First World War in Britain', *Population Studies*, 30 (1976)

4 The Structure of the Economy

During the period under review there were some important changes in the relative importance of various sectors of the economy. Table 8 provides details of the contribution of various sectors of the economy to national income for the census years. The main areas of decline were agricultural, mining, textiles and clothing, rent from dwellings, domestic service and income from abroad. Expanding sectors included engineering together with vehicles, paper and printing, chemicals, gas, electricity and water, building construction, and government and defence services.

For comparative purposes it is convenient to divide the economy into two broad groups: the production and the service sectors. The first of these includes agriculture, mining, construction, electricity, gas and water and manufacturing industry, while the second covers all service trades, public administration, professional activities and transport, but excludes the Armed Forces. The shares of these sectors in terms of output, employment and capital stock are given in Table 9. In 1937 these two sectors were roughly equal in terms of output and employment

Table 8 Distribution of the Gross National Product, 1907–35

	1907	1924	1935
Agriculture, forestry, fishing	6.0	4.2	3.9
Mines and quarries	6.0	5.4	3.1
Engineering and metal manufactures (incl. vehicles)	8.2	8.1	9.4
Textiles and clothing	8.0	7.7	5.6
Food, drink, tobacco	4.3	6.7	5.1
Paper and printing	1.6	2.3	2.6
Chemicals	1.1	1.9	2.1
Miscellaneous manufactures	2.5	3.2	3.5
Gas, electricity, water	1.6	1.7	2.5
Building and construction	3.7	3.1	4.1
Rent of dwellings	7.4	6.4	6.5
Commerce	18.0	17.8	19.6
Transport and communications	9.5	12.0	10.7
Government and defence	3.0	4.6	4.7
Domestic service	3.8	3.4	3.4
Income from abroad	7.2	5.2	4.1
All other, including errors and omissions	8.1	6.3	9.1

Source: P. Deane and W.A. Cole, *British Economic Growth 1688–1959* (Cambridge, 1967), pp. 175, 178

generated, but the service sector accounted for nearly 70 per cent of the total capital stock. Moreover, during the interwar period the latter sector increased its shares of total employment and capital stock, but its share in output declined. This can partly be explained by the fact that some branches of the services, such as domestic service and railway transport, declined in this period, but it also reflects the low level of productivity growth within the sector as a whole. The production sector, on the other

THE STRUCTURE OF THE ECONOMY

Table 9 Shares of Output, Employment and Capital Stock 1924–37 by Sector (Percentages)

	Output 1924	Output 1937	Employment 1924	Employment 1937	Capital 1924	Capital 1937
Agriculture etc.	4.0	3.5	6.2	4.2	5.2	4.1
Mining and quarrying	4.0	3.7	7.4	4.4	3.1	3.7
Manufacturing	28.5	32.8	36.9	35.2	18.0	15.4
Construction	3.4	4.7	4.9	6.1	0.4	0.5
Electricity, gas, water	1.5	2.3	1.2	1.5	6.5	8.3
Goods	42.4	46.9	55.7	51.5	33.2	31.0
Transport and communications	9.4	8.6	8.3	8.0	23.1	20.3
Distributive trades	15.1	14.4	10.2	12.9	11.9	11.4
Other services	27.4	24.6	25.4	27.7	7.7	8.2
Ownership of dwellings	5.7	5.4	–	–	24.0	29.0
Services	57.6	53.1	44.3	48.5	66.7	68.9

Source: J.A. Dowie, 'Growth in the Inter-War Period: Some More Arithmetic', *Economic History Review*, 21 (1968)

hand, increased its share of output, but in terms of employment and capital stock it became smaller. Agriculture, mining and the old staple branches of industry were the main losers.

The growth performance of the main branches in these two sectors are given in Table 10. Despite the importance of the service sector in absorbing resources (that is, capital and manpower) its contribution to the growth of the economy was very modest indeed. In fact output expanded at a rate well below the general average, while a negative residual meant a decline in productivity. On the other hand, since the expansion of services was based on factor inputs rather than improvements in the productivity

Table 10 Annual Rates of Growth of Output, Employment, Capital etc., 1920–38

	Output	Output per man	Employment	Capital	Total factor inputs	Residual
GDP	1.7	1.2	0.5[1]	1.1[2]	0.7	1.0
Agriculture, forestry and fishing	0.9	3.0	−2.1	0.0	−1.5	2.4
Mining and quarrying	0.2	2.5	−2.3	0.7	−1.4	1.6
Construction	5.4	3.6	1.8	1.8	1.8	3.6
Electricity, gas and water	5.0	2.5	2.5	3.3	2.7	2.3
Manufacturing	2.6	2.7	−0.1	0.7	0.1	2.5
All production	2.8	2.9	−0.1	1.4	0.4	2.4
Transport and communication	2.1	2.0	0.1	0.7	0.3	1.8
Distributive trades	1.3	−0.5	1.8	1.3	1.7	−0.4
All services and transport[3]	0.9	−0.7	1.6	1.6	1.6	−0.7

Notes: 1. Excludes Armed Forces
2. Excludes dwellings
3. Includes distributive trades, insurance, banking and finance, public administration, professional and miscellaneous services

Sources: Based on data in K.S. Lomax, 'Production and Productivity Movements in the United Kingdom since 1900', *Journal of the Royal Statistical Society*, A122 (1959); C.H. Feinstein, *Domestic Capital Formation in the United Kingdom, 1920–1938* (Cambridge, 1965), and 'Production and Productivity in the United Kingdom 1920–1962', *London and Cambridge Economic Bulletin*, 48 (1963); A.L. Chapman and R. Knight, *Wages and Salaries in the United Kingdom, 1920–1938* (Cambridge, 1953)

THE STRUCTURE OF THE ECONOMY

of resources, it did mean that employment growth was rapid. Apart from 1921–22, employment in these trades expanded in every year and the group as a whole accounted for the bulk of the increase in employment during the period. Thus at a time of heavy unemployment and large fluctuations in the level of industrial employment, services acted as a stabilising force.

Of course there were considerable variations in the rate of employment growth between the main service trades. The biggest absolute gains occurred in distribution (wholesale and retail) where employment rose from 1773.2 thousand in 1920 to 2438.2 thousand in 1938, and in miscellaneous services, from 2025.4 to 2754.8 thousand. This latter group comprised a wide range of activities including entertainment and sport, catering, laundries and dry cleaning, domestic service and hairdressing. Altogether employment in these two categories rose by nearly 1.4 million. In fact there were few service sectors which failed to register an increase in employment apart from government service, though transport and communications gained only slightly. However, the latter group covered a wide range of transport activities not all of which were expanding. Employment growth was mainly confined to road transport and postal and telegraphic services, while most other branches — railways, tramways, ocean transport and docks — experienced contraction.

In contrast, most of the main industrial groups experienced low rates of employment growth. In fact employment declined in agriculture, mining and manufacturing, and only construction and electricity registered significant gains. Though the rate of expansion was much higher in electricity, gas and water, the absolute increase in employment was much less than in construction. The latter absorbed over 318,000 additional workers between 1920 and 1938 as against 107,000 in electricity etc.

Although the rate of capital growth was lower than pre-war, it was considerably greater than that of employment and most sectors, apart from agriculture, increased their capital stock. The biggest increases were in construction and electricity, while in most of the service sectors, other than transport, it was well above average. On the other hand, in mining, manufacturing and transport the rate of growth of the capital stock was quite modest.

It is clear from the data given in Tables 9 and 10 that there was no clear-cut association between growth of output and the expansion of factor inputs (capital and labour). It is true that the two sectors with the highest rate of output growth — construction and electricity — also had the highest input growth, though in the case of construction this accounted for only one third of the rise in output. But here the positive association ends, for in most other sectors growth and factor inputs tended to be inversely correlated. Thus the service sectors, other than transport, had a high input growth but a relatively modest increase in output, while productivity declined. On the other hand, manufacturing and transport, with low rates of factor input, recorded a creditable performance in output and productivity. Even mining and agriculture, where inputs declined sharply, did very well in terms of productivity.

The distinction between the two main sectors of the economy is, therefore, quite meaningful. Services provided the main source of increased employment, but their contribution to the growth of output and productivity was rather limited. The reverse was true of the industrial sector of the economy. Here input growth was very modest but output and productivity expanded much faster than the economy as a whole. Thus from the point of view of the overall growth of the economy the industrial sector was by far the more important.

Study Questions on the Structure of the Economy

(a) Discuss the main changes in the structure of the economy between the wars.

(b) What contribution did the service sector make to the interwar economy?

(c) Examine the differences in productivity growth of the main sectors of the economy.

Recommended Reading on the Structure of the Economy

Allen, G.C., *The Structure of Industry in Britain* (London, 1963)

Dunning, J.H. and Thomas, C.J., *British Industry: Change and Development in the Twentieth Century* (London, 1961)

Deane, P. and Cole, W.A., *British Economic Growth, 1688–1959* (Cambridge, 1967)

5 Agriculture

Before 1914 Britain was largely dependent on foreign supplies to feed the nation. The war brought with it U-boat attacks on British mercantile ships, causing Britain to look to the home market for the production of the necessary food requirements. To achieve this independence, concentration was placed on encouraging increased cultivation of economically-produced, high calorie foods such as cereals and potatoes, at the expense of 'luxury' or non-essential crops such as hops. In 1917 the introduction of the Corn Production Act meant guaranteed high minimum cereal prices for farmers. Other influences such as minimum wages for agricultural workers, prisoner-of-war labour and a Women's Land Army led to fairly satisfactory results, as shown in Table 11.

Immediate postwar conditions were favourable for agriculture, since minimum prices and wages were still guaranteed. However, after 1920 there was a general slump in world agriculture prices, especially in cereals; the price of wheat, for example, fell by more than one half between 1920 and 1922. Since it could no longer afford to subsidise crops at these low prices, the government

Table 11 Changes in Production Occasioned by World War I

	1909–13	1918
Wheat (million qtrs.)	7.0	11.6
Oats (million qtrs.)	21.6	31.5
Potatoes (million qtrs.)	6.5	9.2
Milk (million gallons)	1,900.0	1,500.0
Beef and Mutton (million tons)	1.0	0.85

Source: W. Johnson, J. Whyman and G. Wykes, *A Short Economic and Social History of Twentieth Century Britain*, (London, 1968), p. 37

adopted its prewar laissez-faire attitude by repealing the Corn Production Acts of 1917 and 1920. The natural tendency then was for agriculture to swing back to its prewar state, and to concentrate on fruit, dairy produce and meat production. This added to the already increasing number of unemployed, since pasture requires from seven to nine men less per thousand acres than arable land, and naturally farmers wanted those types of farming which yielded a high return per man. Although home demand for these goods rose, falling costs abroad and more efficient methods of packing, grading and preserving meant fierce foreign competition. Faced with these burdens, agriculture turned into a declining and generally depressed industry.

The government tried to relieve the situation in various ways. It continued the prewar encouragement of small holdings by introducing several acts: in 1919, the Land Settlement (Facilities) Act, whereby 17,000 ex-servicemen were settled on farms; in 1926, the Small Holding and Allotments Act and in 1931, the agricultural Land (Utilisation) Act, both of which allowed subsidies to be given to County Councils which let small holdings. These Acts proved fairly unsuccessful.

Other measures included the provision of substantial credits by the Agricultural Credits Act of 1928 and the relief of agricultural land and buildings from the burden of rates in 1929. However, these could do little to shield agriculture from the onslaught of the depression, 1929–33, when world prices fell dramatically.

The most significant result of government aid in the 1920s was the introduction of the sugar beet industry into the UK. The British Sugar Subsidy Act of 1925 ensured a subsidy for ten years, with the eventual aim of self-reliance. Between 1925 and 1935, the output of sugar beet rose from 431 tons to 3,404 tons and remained fairly stable after that. The high costs of this venture led to the establishment of a central body, the British Sugar Corporation, and a Sugar Commission to supervise research, etc. This helped to stabilise the industry and good results were achieved.

The government was forced to assist agriculture more extensively in the critical years of the depression. It did so by introducing the Agricultural Marketing Acts of 1931 and 1933, the Wheat Act of 1932 and the Import Duties Act of 1932. The Agricultural Marketing Acts provided for the creation of boards, by at least two thirds of the producers of any agricultural product, for the purpose of rationalising marketing methods. Boards for products such as potatoes, milk, pigs and bacon were established. The Wheat Act meant that producers were guaranteed a standard price of 10s per cwt. A ceiling limit to the subsidy granted would discourage production in an already overstocked world.

Despite all these measures, British agriculture remained depressed. Migration from the land to the cities increased. The proportion of the workforce engaged in agriculture declined steadily over the interwar period from 6.2 to 4.2 per cent (1924–37). During the same period agriculture's share of total domestic output fell from 4.0 to 3.5 per cent. The decline in the labour force was particularly marked in the 1930s when employment in agriculture (excluding farmers) declined from 742,000 in 1930 to 593,000 in 1938. The number of farmers however remained fairly stable throughout the whole interwar period at round 225,000. Also, the change from arable to pasture farming continued. By 1937–38, livestock and livestock products accounted for 70.5 per cent of the value of agricultural output, with farm crops and horticultural products accounting for 16.1 and 13.4 per cent respectively. Britain maintained a fair degree of self-sufficiency in several products, notably liquid milk, potatoes, pigmeat, vegetables, poultry and eggs. Nevertheless the bulk of Britain's food supplies were drawn from abroad, since for the more easily transported commodities such as beef, mutton, lamb, cereals, fruits, flour and sugar, the dependence on foreign sources of supply was substantial. The cost to the state of subsidies was so large that it would possibly have been cheaper to import even more food supplies. However, agricultural output did rise by about one sixth in volume between 1931 and 1937, mainly due to increased labour productivity. In fact, productivity in agriculture rose quite rapidly during the interwar period (see Table 10) as a result of the sharp reduction in the labour force, the spread of mechanisation and the adoption of new techniques and management methods.

The benefits of state intervention were not realised fully until World War II broke out. Once again Britain had to rely on domestic production. This necessitated, as in the First World War, a change from pasture to arable land, which was aided in 1939 by a government subsidy of £2 per acre for ploughing land which had lain unploughed for seven years or more. As a result, the arable land area increased from under 12 million to 18 million acres and this was accompanied by substantial increases in yields of grain crops (see Table 12).

Table 12 Productivity of Grain Acreage

Yield/acre	1936–38 (cwt)	1942–45 (cwt)
Wheat	17.7	19.7
Barley	16.4	18.5
Oats	15.7	16.7

During the war, net output of British agriculture increased by about 35 per cent. This was achieved by a rapid increase in mechanisation so that by the end of the hostilities British agriculture was among the most highly mechanised in the world. The process of adapting to war needs was under the direct control of the County War Agricultural Committees, which stipulated land use, allocation of labour, machinery and other resources to achieve the desired results. The government also provided subsidies for improvement schemes. More labour was required for arable land and so to prevent the shift out of agriculture, wages were increased substantially. Much of the administration needed to run such a direct programme in agriculture during hostilities was in fact already in existence before the war. All these facets meant that results were more than favourable, not only in providing the nation with the necessary commodities, but also in building up the industry itself. The Second World War was a period of recovery and expansion for British agriculture.

Study Questions on Agriculture

(a) How did the First World War affect British agriculture?
(b) Why did agriculture decline after 1920?
(c) What assistance did the government offer to British agriculture in the interwar years?

Recommended Reading on Agriculture

Walworth, G., *Feeding the Nation in Peace and War* (London, 1940)
Whetham, E.H., *The Agrarian History of England and Wales*, Vol. 8, *1914–39* (Cambridge, 1978)

6 Industrial Production

Given the importance of the contribution of the industrial sector to the growth of the economy it is important to look more closely at the changes taking place in this sector. The more vigorous growth of the interwar years compared with before 1914 may be explained to a large extent by the technical advances and economies of scale associated with the structural changes taking place within the economy, and more particularly those in the industrial sector. This is in contrast to the period before 1914 when there were relatively few significant structural changes in the pattern of activity. By and large the expansion of the economy then depended upon the continued development of existing sectors. This was especially true in the case of the industrial sector which accounted for around 45 per cent of total output. A few large staple industries dominated the field. In 1907 coal, textiles, iron and steel and engineering (including shipbuilding) accounted for 50 per cent of net industrial output, they employed about one quarter of the occupied labour force and supplied 70 per cent of Britain's exports. Resources continued to be poured into these industries despite the fact that their rate of expansion (especially productivity) slackened in the couple of decades before the war. Low productivity growth was largely a function of the slow rate of technical advance, while developments in new, high growth sectors based on inventions such as electricity and the internal combustion engine, were very limited. By 1907 the newer industries (electrical engineering, road vehicles, rayon, chemicals and scientific instruments) accounted for only 6.5 of net industrial output and 5.2 per cent of industrial employment. Thus as far as industry was concerned the shift of resources from low to high growth sectors was very limited. The service sectors — transport, finance, distribution etc. — expanded quite rapidly at least in terms of employment, and in this respect some of them increased in relative importance. But rates of output and productivity growth in the service trades were relatively low and could not offset the retardation in the industrial sector.

In other words, before 1914 Britain's resources tended to be concentrated in slow-growing sectors with a low rate of technical advance, while large-scale innovations, especially those giving rise to new industries, were slow to mature. Inter-sectoral shifts of resources tended to be between low productivity sectors rather than from low to high growth sectors. The contrast with the postwar situation is quite marked. In the first place, the export-predominant, staple industries declined in importance and gave way to new industries, which expanded rapidly by exploiting new techniques and reaping economies of scale. In 1935 the new industries accounted for 21 per cent of net industrial output compared with 14.1 per cent in 1924 and 6.5 per cent in 1907. This calculation takes no account of electricity supply which expanded very rapidly indeed. Secondly, the construction and allied trades expanded rapidly compared with prewar, largely as a result of the massive housebuilding programme.

A comparative analysis for 21 industry groups is given in Table 13. From this the division between the old and new industrial sectors can be appreciated readily. The fastest growers, that is those with a rate of growth of output above the average for all industry, included three new

INDUSTRIAL PRODUCTION

Table 13 Annual Rates of Growth of Output, Employment, Capital, etc., in Selected Industries 1920–38

	Output	Output per man	Employment	Capital	Total	Residual
Vehicles	6.6	3.6	3.0	5.4	3.7	2.9
Building and contracting	5.4	3.6	1.8	1.8	1.8	3.6
Timber and furniture	5.2	5.0	0.2	–	–	–
Electricity, gas, water	5.0	2.5	2.5	3.3	2.7	2.3
Non-ferrous metal manufacture	4.8	3.6	1.2	1.4	1.3	3.5
Electrical engineering	4.7	1.1	3.6	2.3	3.2	1.5
Building materials	3.7	1.6	2.1	−0.5	1.3	2.4
Food	3.6	2.1	1.5	0.6	1.2	2.4
Clothing	2.7	2.9	−0.2	2.3	0.8	1.9
Precision instruments	2.7	3.0	−0.3	–	–	–
Paper and printing	2.6	1.3	1.3	2.0	1.5	1.1
Metal goods	2.5	2.1	0.4	–	–	–
Tobacco	2.2	1.7	0.5	2.4	1.1	1.1
Leather	2.1	2.3	−0.2	2.2	0.5	1.8
Chemicals	1.9	1.5	0.4	1.4	0.7	1.2
Mechanical engineering	1.7	3.7	−2.0	0.3	−1.3	3.0
Iron and steel	1.1	3.5	−2.4	0.7	−1.5	2.6
Textiles	0.2	1.6	−1.4	−0.9	−1.3	1.5
Mining and quarrying	0.2	2.5	−2.3	0.7	−1.4	1.6
Drink	−0.2	−1.0	0.8	0.4	0.7	−0.9
Shipbuilding	−2.7	1.9	−4.6	−0.8	−3.4	0.7
Manufacturing	2.6	2.7	−0.1	0.7	0.1	2.5
All industry (excl. agric.)	2.8	2.9	−0.1	1.4	0.4	2.4

Note: (a) This is the measure of output per unit of labour and capital; in other words the productivity of factors of production, or that part of growth not attributable to capital and labour inputs.

Sources: as for Table 10

industries — vehicles, electricity and electrical engineering — together with building and allied trades, food and non-ferrous metals. Moreover, all these industries had high rates of employment and total input growth. However, rapid expansion did not necessarily produce high rates of productivity growth. Productivity rose at a rate below the average in four of the eight industries at the top of Table 13 and two of these — electricity and electrical engineering — were new industries.

At the other end of the scale six industries had rates of output growth well below the average. These comprised mechanical engineering, iron and steel, textiles, mining, drink and shipbuilding, most of which were affected badly by adverse world market conditions. In textiles and mining there was virtually no expansion, while drink and shipbuilding actually contracted over the period 1920–38. The textile group however covers a number of different branches, some of which expanded. Unfortunately full details are not available for each branch, but employment data show that the declining areas were cotton, woollen and worsted products, linen, hemp and jute, whereas rayon, silk and hosiery expanded. In addition, in most of these industries the growth of employment and capital was very modest. There were, too, some sharp variations in productivity growth. Productivity rose rapidly in iron and steel and mechanical engineering, and even in mining, shipbuilding and textiles it was by no means negligible. In fact, of all the industries listed, only drink recorded a negative rate of productivity growth.

Finally, in the middle range, that is those with a rate of output growth around or below the average (between 1.9 and 2.7 per cent per annum) there were seven industries. These included both old consumer goods industries such as clothing, leather and tobacco and newer trades like chemicals and precision instruments. Most of the industries in this class also had fairly low rates of productivity growth apart from precision instruments. On the other hand, four of the industries — paper and printing, tobacco, metal goods and chemicals — had employment growth rates above the average.

John Brown's Shipyard, Clydebank, Glasgow in 1931, when work stopped on the Cunarder 534 (Queen Mary) for lack of funds. Shipbuilding was one of the old staple industries whose rate of growth was well below average in the interwar years.

What importance should be attached to the newer industries? Recently their role in the interwar economy has been stressed, particularly with reference to the recovery phase of the 1930s.[1] There is of course a danger of exaggerating their contribution, since although all new industries were expanding, not all expanding industries were new ones. It can be seen from Table 13 that nearly all industries could be classed as expanding both in terms of output and productivity, though not necessarily from the employment point of view. The only exceptions were drink and shipbuilding. In other words, it could be argued that interwar industrial growth was fairly widely based. On the other hand, it is equally clear that the large staple industries acted as a drag on overall growth, though a few achieved reasonable rates of productivity growth. At the top end of the scale it could hardly be said that new industries predominated. Only three of the fastest output growers were new industries, while the performance of chemicals and precision instruments was rather mediocre. Moreover, in terms of productivity growth the comparison is even less favourable to the new industries. Only two, vehicles and precision instruments, were above the average, and the ranking of the first eight was as follows: timber and furniture, mechanical engineering, vehicles, building and contracting, non-ferrous metal manufacture, iron and steel, precision instruments and clothing.

Without stretching the evidence too far therefore, we might suggest that industrial development was centred primarily on two interrelated blocks of industries. On the one hand, there were the new industries, especially vehicles, electricity and electrical engineering, but also including rayon, chemicals and precision instruments; on the other, we have the building and allied trades (timber, furniture, building materials and non-ferrous metals). Construction was more important than any of the newer industries taken separately. In terms of output and

---

1. For a review see N.K. Buxton, 'The Role of the New Industries in Britain During the 1930s: A Reinterpretation', *Business History Review*, 44 (Summer 1975).

employment it was twice as large as electricity (including gas and water), which was the biggest branch of the newer group of activities.

There are at least three good reasons for stressing the importance of these sectors. First, nearly all of them expanded rapidly either in terms of output or productivity and they absorbed an increasing share of the resources devoted to industry. Building and related trades gave employment to some 1364.1 thousand people in 1920 and 1795.2 thousand in 1938, while in the newer industries employment rose from 981.8 to 1582.2 thousand over the same period. These two sectors combined accounted for 30.5 per cent of the total industrial labour force in 1920, 37.4 in 1929, and 42.2 per cent in 1938. They were also responsible for over 60 per cent of total investment in the UK during the interwar years.

Secondly, their expansion exerted a considerable impact on other sectors, since many of them had a relatively high volume of transactions with other industries. This was especially true of vehicles, electricity, electrical engineering and building. To take an obvious example: the development of the motor car industry stimulated or brought into being a wide range of industries, including oil refining, rubber, electrical goods, glass, leather, metallurgy and mechanical engineering. The strongest repercussions came from the building industry. Altogether it bought products from 24 out of 36 main industry groups and the total inter-industry transactions on behalf of this industry amounted to nearly £213 million. The main industries from which products were drawn included china and glass, oils and paints, iron and steel manufactures, metal goods, non-ferrous metals, wood manufacturers, mechanical engineering, and of course building materials. Though the total inter-industry transactions of the building industry were small in relation to industrial production as a whole, what is important is that only two other industries — food processing and distribution services — had a greater volume of transactions with other industries.

Thus the new industries and the building trades not only generated a demand for each other's products but they also exerted a favourable influence on some of the old staple industries, particularly iron and steel, mechanical engineering, metal goods and certain branches of the textile trades. The third point to note is that the building trades and new industries were by no means independent development blocks. Though the transactions between the two sectors were perhaps not so great as those between different branches within each of the two groups, the indirect repercussions were considerable. The building of over four million new houses in the interwar period could not fail to exert a significant impact on other sectors of the economy. Not only did it stimulate a demand for a wide variety of community services such as schools, shops, churches and other public utilities, but since most of the new houses were wired for electricity it generated a demand for a wide range of new consumer durables based on the new form of power. By 1939 there were already in use some 1.6 million electric cookers, 2.3 million vacuum cleaners, 6.5 million electric irons and nearly 0.5 million electric water heaters. The demand for many other household goods was likewise stimulated by the housebuilding programme. Furthermore, residential building stimulated the development of new transport facilities, while in turn the flexibility, convenience and relative cheapness of motor transport enabled new building to take place in the suburbs of the main industrial cities.

Although we may say fairly confidently that the long-term growth of the economy was carried forward by building and the newer industries, this does not mean that they were equally important during different phases of the cycle. Given the fact that they were proportionately more important in the 1930s than in the previous decade, one would naturally expect their contribution to be greater in this period. Between 1924 and 1935 the proportion of net output of all census of production trades accounted for by the new industries rose from 14.1 to 21.0 per cent. House construction accounted for the bulk of net capital formation (i.e. net additions to the capital stock) and its share of capital in GNP rose from 2.3 in the 1920s to 3.4 per cent in 1930–38. In the first half of the 1930s this was certainly the case, since recovery from the depression was determined largely by the early and powerful upswing in these sectors. But in the later phase of revival the growth momentum of both the building trades and the newer industries tended to slacken, while at the same time some of the older staple trades began to make their contribution to recovery.

The position is much less clear-cut in the 1920s. In one sense it could be argued that these newer sectors were of vital importance simply because of the rather sluggish rates of growth experienced in some of the other industries. This is particularly true of the later 1920s when the negative or very low rates of expansion in iron and steel, textiles, mining and shipbuilding, were responsible for the dampened nature of the boom. During these years most of the new industries, and for a time the building trades, registered very high rates of expansion. On the other hand, in terms of productivity the position was more varied. Some of the older industries, such as mining and shipbuilding, had quite high rates of productivity growth, whereas the reverse was true in the case of certain new industries, notably chemicals and electrical engineering. When we turn to the early 1920s it is less easy to make out a convincing case for these sectors. The boom of 1919–20 was clearly one based on the old staples and they were instrumental in causing the subsequent slump. In the ensuing recovery both old and new industries expanded rapidly though building, which had acted as a stabilising influence in 1921, actually contracted until 1923. Moreover, the new industries could hardly have exerted a powerful influence in these years since their relative importance was still quite small. In particular, it is scarcely conceivable that they were responsible for the rapid rise in industrial productivity between 1920–24, which was at the rate of 5.6 per cent per annum. To some extent this rather high rate reflected the low level of productivity attained at the end of the war, but it was also due to the adoption of more efficient methods of production in some trades, notably engineering. More important however, was the shake-out of labour from many of the older industries which had been grossly overmanned before the war. Thus the output of the mechanical engineering industry rose by six per cent between 1920–24, yet the labour force was reduced by no less than 46 per cent. Similarly, there was a 19 per cent expansion in the output of mining and quarrying despite the fact that employment fell slightly.

Study Questions on Industrial Production

(a) Is it useful to make a distinction between the 'new' and 'old' industries?
(b) What caused the decline of the staple industries after 1920?
(c) Examine the contribution of building and the new industries to the economic recovery of the 1930s.

Recommended Reading on Industrial Production

Alford, B.W.E., 'New Industries for Old? British Industry between the Wars', in R. Floud and D. McCloskey (eds), *The Economic History of Britain since 1700*, Vol. 2, *1860 to the 1970s* (Cambridge, 1981)

Buxton, N.K. and Aldcroft, D.H. (eds), *British Industry between the Wars* (London, 1979)

Richardson, H.W., 'The New Industries between the Wars', *Oxford Economic Papers*, 13 (1961)

7 Industrial Structure and Business Organisation

The changes in industrial composition outlined above were reflected in the geographical pattern of activity. The staple industries tended to be concentrated in the northern regions of the country with the result that as these sectors declined in importance so did the economic importance of the regions in which they were situated. Conversely, the tendency for the newer industries or rapidly expanding trades to concentrate in the South and Midlands raised the importance of these areas. Thus between 1924 and 1935 the northern regions' share of net industrial output fell from 49.6 to 37.6 per cent, whereas the share of the Southeast and the Midlands rose from 28.7 to 37.1 per cent.

Changes in the pattern and form of business organisation, which affected old and new industries alike, were less spectacular but nonetheless important. These included the widespread use of the corporate form of enterprise, the development of public and semi-public undertakings, the increase in the size of plant and firm and a vast extension in the number of trade associations or cartel-like arrangements for price fixing, information sharing, distribution etc. Most of these changes simply represented extensions of developments which had been going on since before 1914. The joint-stock company, for example, had been in widespread use long before the war, though there were still many individually owned firms or partnerships in business. Many of these undertakings converted to corporate form in the interwar period and by 1938 the majority of industrial firms were joint-stock companies. Even so, non-corporate concerns were still to be found quite frequently in retail distribution, in road transport and in many of the small trades. The extension of this form of business organisation usually reflected the need to draw in larger amounts of capital from a wider field, though many companies fell short of a stock exchange quotation. In fact, the number of public companies declined during the period despite the fact that many private firms became public, while in numerical terms private companies were far more important. The latter were usually small and in aggregate they accounted for less than one third of the total capital of all joint-stock enterprises. Nevertheless, the effect of incorporation, whether of a private or public type, led to an increasing divorce between ownership and control in many firms. Certainly most of the larger companies were managed by executives and directors answerable to a large body of shareholders.

Private enterprise was not alone in the economic field. One of the notable features of the period was the increasing economic participation of the state, which, if we include local authorities, accounted for between 25 and 30 per cent of total national expenditure. Of course, a very large part of this expenditure went on transfer payments, [1] defence and direct government purchases, so that the proportion of economic property owned or directly controlled by state organs was very much smaller that these figures suggest. Nevertheless, direct participation was increasing as both central and local authorities extended

---

1. Payments made by the state in the form of pensions, unemployment benefits etc., for which there is no productive contribution to the flow of goods and services.

INDUSTRIAL STRUCTURE AND BUSINESS ORGANISATION

their spheres of influence. Local authorities, for example, had large stakes in gas, water and electricity and in road transport including tramways, together with a host of smaller trading activities. In addition, there were many semi-public utilities such as dock and harbour authorities in which local government participated. The Central Government's interests were less extensive but again increasing. To the Post Office and naval dockyards, which had been controlled by the State for centuries, were added the administration of several new public or semi-public corporations, notably the Forestry Commission (1919), the Central Electricity Board (1926), the British Broadcasting Corporation (1926), the London Passenger Transport Board (1933) and British Overseas Airways Corporation (1939). Indirectly, of course, the State's influence was much greater, since in this period it sought to control or regulate the activities of a wide range of industries. This was especially true in the 1930s when the government sought to regulate or protect many industries, for example coal, cotton and road transport, which were either in distress or which competed with the old staple industries.

A further feature of the industrial structure was the tendency for firms and plants to increase in size in terms of output and employment. This was caused both by amalgamation and natural growth. Nearly every industry and trade was affected in some way by amalgamation (either horizontal or vertical) and this often resulted in a fairly high degree of concentration and/or complex interconnections between different industries. Thus over 100 railway companies were welded into four large groups in the early 1920s, Imperial Chemical Industries, formed in 1926 from four main firms in the industry, acquired control of more than one third of the British chemical output, while in some of the older industries a complex set of inter-industry holding arrangements (various forms of cross-ownership operations) was formed in this period. It is difficult to give any precise measure of the changes in size and concentration either at the plant or firm level, since comprehensive data on the size structure of industry is not available before the Census of Production in 1935. An additional difficulty is that there are a number of ways of measuring size, for example by employment, capital or output, not all of which produce the same results. There seems little doubt, however, that concentration of economic activity was increasing during this period. On the basis of the Factory Inspectors' reports, Sargent Florence estimated that the mean size of plant in manufacturing rose from 16.5 to 23.5 persons between 1904 and 1938, while by 1935, 10 per cent of the largest British plants employed 76 per cent of all persons in factories of 100 or more employees, a proportion similar to that of the United States.[2] In fact over one half of the workers enumerated in the 1935 Census worked in industrial units employing 500 men or more and some of the most highly concentrated plants were to be found in mining, aircraft manufacture, tramways, biscuit-making, iron and steel, and the railways. A study made by Leak and Maizels on the basis of the 1935 Census suggests that the concentration of output was very high indeed in some fields, especially in the new industries.[3] For example, the percentage of net output accounted for by the three largest units in any one industry was 84 per cent in rayon and dyestuffs, 75 per cent in photographic apparatus, 73 per cent in rubber tyres and tubes, 66 per cent in electric wires and cables and aluminium, 48 per cent in electrical machinery and 45 per cent in motor car manufacture. In some cases the process of concentration had occurred primarily after the war. By contrast concentration ratios in many of the staple industries were much lower: in iron and steel blast furnaces 34 per cent, shipbuilding 27 per cent, cotton spinning 26 per cent, iron and steel smelting and rolling 21 per cent, and brewing 18 per cent. At the extreme lower end of the spectrum a number of industries had percentages of less than 10, including mechanical engineering, woollen and worsted manufacture, furniture, leather, clothing, cotton weaving, and building contracting. On the other hand,

---

2. P. Sargent Florence, *The Logic of British and American Industry* (London, 1953), pp. 31–5.
3. H. Leak and A. Maizels, 'The Structure of British Industry', *Journal of the Royal Statistical Society*, 108 (1945).

there were a number of trades, few of which could be classed as new, where one firm or group controlled 70 per cent or more of capacity. Some of these, such as textile finishing, sewing cotton, wallpaper, Portland cement and flat glass, had originated in the prewar period, while others came to dominate their markets as a result of mergers and absorptions of competing firms in the interwar years, the most notable examples being whisky distilling, soap and margarine, matches, glass bottles and seed crushing.

The trend towards concentration and the reduction of competition were reinforced by the widespread adoption of trade associations. These had been common before the war, though many new ones were formed in response to government control during the period of hostilities. Most of these were continued afterwards and in the hard market environment of the interwar period trade associations flourished for the purposes of restricting competition and stabilising prices. By the late 1930s there were probably over 1000 in manufacturing alone. Many of these were very loose associations which provided information on prices, sales and other matters to their constituent members. Others, however, had very elaborate restrictive agreements covering prices, output and sales and were more akin to the German cartel-type of organisation. The Cable Makers' Association, for example, which covered 90 per cent of total production, controlled the prices and output of the member firms and operated a system of allocating orders on a quota basis. The electrical products and building materials industries were riddled with restrictive agreements some of which were very rigid indeed. But private enterprise was not solely responsible for the growth of associations and agreements. The government was instrumental in sponsoring many trade associations during the war in order to facilitate the control of industry, while in the 1930s it encouraged the formation of cartel-like arrangements of producer organisations in an effort to curtail competition and bolster up industries in distress. The policy of the government was an important factor in the acceptance of control in some industries including coal, shipbuilding, iron and steel, agriculture, herring fishing and tramp shipping. In addition, the state sought to eliminate or reduce competition by subsidies, tariffs and restrictive legislation as in the case of civil aviation, iron and steel, beet sugar and road transport.

Reasons for the trends in business organisation are not difficult to find. Market and technical factors tended to favour the growth in size of units and as the latter increased it naturally affected the type of firm structure. The non-incorporated one-man business or family partnership became increasingly unsuitable as the technical complexity of modern production increased. In some industries, motor car manufacturing in particular, large firms or units of production were essential if the benefits of mass production were to be reaped. There were, of course, still many small firms or businesses and, although a large number either failed or were absorbed by larger concerns, the ranks were continually being filled by new entrants. Numerically small firms predominated, but in terms of output and employment they played a minor role. The existence of so many small enterprises was not only due to the tenacity or independence of individual owners, though this no doubt was an important factor. For some branches of production, such as machine tools and boot and shoe manufacturing, small or medium sized firms tended to predominate simply because they were the optimum. In addition to these factors, competition and the uncertain conditions of the period forced firms to cooperate or merge their interests and encouraged the development of restrictive arrangements in one form or another.

Study Questions on Industrial Structure and Business Organisation

(a) What changes took place in business organisation in the interwar years?

(b) Why did concentration in industry increase during the period?

(c) How did the government influence industrial structure?

Recommended Reading on Industrial Structure and Business Organisation

Beacham, A., *Structure of British Industry* (London, 1955)

Dunning, J.H. and Thomas, W.A., *British Industry* (London, 1961)

Hannah, L., 'Managerial Innovation and the Rise of the Large-scale Company in Interwar Britain', *Economic History Review*, 27 (1974)

Hannah, L., *The Rise of the Corporate Economy* (London, 1976)

8 Transport and Communications

The First World War can be seen as something of a watershed in the history of transport, since in the years that followed the changes in the pattern of development were more rapid than before 1914. There was however a marked contrast between sectors. Most of the old established forms of transport — railways, canals, shipping and tramways — either stagnated or declined, whereas previously they had been growing steadily. On the other hand, motor transport and civil aviation expanded rapidly (though the latter only accounted for a small share of expenditure on transport by the end of the period).

Output data for transport suggest that this sector grew fairly rapidly between 1913 and 1920 through to 1938, though there was some slowing up in the rate of expansion in the mid-1930s. Private consumers' expenditure on passenger transport (at constant 1938 prices) almost doubled between 1920 and 1938 and the share of this sector (including communications) in total spending rose from 3.8 per cent before the war to 6.5 per cent in 1925–29 and to 7.5 per cent in 1935–38.

The percentage increase in expenditure on private

The International Motor Show at Olympia, London, in the late 1920s. The interwar years saw a dramatic increase in private motoring and vehicle manufacturing was one of the new industries with an above-average productivity growth.

motoring was quite phenomenal. By 1938 expenditure on the purchase and running of vehicles (including motor cycles) had risen to just over £135 million as against £179 million spent on public transport. In the latter sector it was again road transport which set the pace and by the end of the period expenditure on this branch was nearly double that on rail. Most of the increase went on bus and coach travel, since all other forms of road transport — tramways, taxis and horse-drawn vehicles — declined in importance. Expenditure on rail travel managed a modest rise through to 1938 but, unlike road transport, there were some quite sharp downturns, notably between 1929 and 1932. Expenditure on shipping services declined quite sharply, whereas that on air transport rose steadily, though even by 1938 it amounted to only £0.5 million.

The expenditure data may tend to be misleading since short-distance journeys involved a high price per passenger mile. Hence information on passenger miles travelled perhaps gives a better idea of the relative distribution between different modes. In 1920 passenger miles travelled by rail accounted for about 60 per cent of the total passenger mileage by public transport, while the share of bus and coach travel was not much more than 10 per cent and tramways and trolleybuses accounted for one quarter. By 1938 buses and coaches accounted for almost as many passenger miles as the railways whose share of the total had fallen to 42 per cent. A rough estimate for private car travel in 1938 suggests that passenger miles amounted to one half the total for all forms of public transport.

Thus, in the interwar period, motor transport became a very serious rival to existing forms of inland transport. On the freight side, the same process was taking place, though less severely since the railways retained their monopoly of the carriage of heavy bulky products. The individual sectors may now be considered in turn.

The main factors working against the railways were the stagnation in traffic, the growth of road competition and the cost-price structure of the system. Not only was there an overall stagnation in traffic levels, but quite severe contractions in both passenger and goods traffic occurred in 1920–21, 1925–26, 1929–32 and 1937–38, years characterised by sharp recessions in economic activity generally. The overall trend in freight traffic was sharply downward, while passenger traffic held up rather better; in terms of passenger miles there was a slight increase in traffic. Unfortunately the railways retained a monopoly in the very branches of traffic which were in secular decline — the products of the heavy staple industries, coal, iron, steel, shipbuilding and textiles — which the railway network had been designed to serve in the nineteenth century. The loss recorded in coal traffic was considerable from 225.5 million tons in 1913 to 188.2 million in 1937, and in 1933 it had receded to as low as 165.4 million tons.

The rapid growth of motor transport undoubtedly posed a serious problem for the railways. There was a great burst of expansion in the years immediately following the war. This growth was assisted by the release of many ex-army vehicles onto the market. After the early 1920s the rate of expansion slowed down somewhat though it still remained at a high level. Rapid advances were made in the methods of producing vehicles and in their technical performance. Mass production was largely accomplished during the 1920s. The introduction of the diesel engine meant savings for operators with high annual mileages, such as public service vehicles and the larger road haulage vehicles. From the economic point of view the most important technical innovation was the introduction of the pneumatic tyre, which reduced the running costs of vehicles considerably. Such improvements soon enabled the bus to emerge as a rival to the tram and later the railway. Overall the effect of these advances was to reduce considerably both the capital and running costs of motor vehicles and this in turn widened the market. By 1939 motoring was no longer a luxury confined to the rich.

The railways lost quite a considerable amount of traffic to their competitors, the bulk of these losses occurring in passenger traffic and merchandise freight. On the revenue side the railways pricing policy did not help matters. During the interwar years, the railways were caught in the awkward position of having rather inflexible costs at a time when prices (including their charges) were moving downwards. Since their competitors' charges were falling it was not always possible to raise rates to match costs, though a more rational pricing policy would have alleviated the problem to some extent. Given the failure on this score the only option open to the railways was to secure cost reductions via economies in operation or through technical innovation. The railways did in fact achieve considerable cost savings in one form or another as a result of the better utilisation of their resources and without these, net returns would have been very poor indeed.

Flying was technically possible by 1914 but it was very unreliable, dangerous and costly; consequently there were no commercial air services worth speaking of. Under the stimulus of war, technical advancement was rapid so that by the end of the hostilities regular flying was more feasible. Attempts to provide services to the Continent were shortlived since returns were poor and operations were unprofitable. In 1924 the government established Imperial Airways, which took over the four private companies then in existence.

Within the first decade the company had regular air links with India, Africa and Australia. Small, unsafe, high cost, single-engined planes of pre-Imperial days were replaced by safer, faster, multi-engined aircraft. During the period 1924–34, Imperial Airways extended its route mileage from 1,520 to 15,529, while passenger traffic increased from 10,321 to 66,324. It is important to note that without subsidies the airline company would have run at a loss. In 1935, British Airways was set up to take over the main independent operators on the European network. The two companies were merged into one public undertaking, British Overseas Airways Corporation, at the beginning of the war.

Apart from the feeder services of Imperial Airways, there were virtually no regular air services operated within Britain before the early 1930s. Retarding factors included government refusal to subsidise internal routes, the limited number of decent aerodromes, and the poor quality and high operating costs of the early aircraft. Given the technical limitations of aircraft, flying could not offer time and cost savings over ground transport.

By the early 1930s many of these factors had changed for the better and a whole host of companies came into being largely to service the domestic market. By the middle of the decade a network of regular services had been established and altogether some 20 concerns operated about 76 different services. The business was far from profitable however. Adverse climatic conditions and inadequate facilities made for a rather erratic service. Often ground transport was more reliable and faster than air.

Aviation was still in the pioneer stage commercially by the end of the interwar period. It was still only a marginal supplier of transport services both in the passenger and freight markets. Thus surface operators, both on land and sea, experienced no real competitive threat from this newcomer until after 1945.

The branch of transport which suffered most in the period was that of overseas shipping. After a spectacular postwar boom, when freight rates and ship prices rocketed, there were few really prosperous years for British shipowners. Freight rates and profits were either stagnant or declining for most of the time. The worst years were the early 1930s at the time of the world slump. A slow recovery took place in the later 1930s, but even in the best year (1937–38) prosperity was still some way below the immediate prewar years.

The chief problem in the maritime world after the war was the large amount of tonnage surplus to requirements, as a result of the rapid increase in the size of foreign fleets, the improved technical performance of new ships, and the sluggish growth in seaborne trade. By the early 1930s world seaborne trade was about the same as in 1913 whereas the volume of tonnage was nearly 50 per cent higher. The size of the British fleet declined slightly at a time when world tonnage rose by 46 per cent (1913–38), so that Britain's share of world tonnage declined from 42.8 to 26.0 per cent. The sharp fall of British exports, especially coal, the decline in emigrant traffic, and the growth of subsidised foreign fleets, were only partly to blame for Britain's loss of share. Perhaps equally important was the marked conservatism of Britain's shipowners in their reluctance to adapt to changing conditions; in particular, the slowness with which they exploited new trades, for example the oil market, or adopted new innovations such as diesel propulsion. The more dynamic Scandinavian shipowners, for example, fared rather better than their British counterparts in the interwar period.

The three categories of postal services, namely correspondence, parcels and remittance services, varied somewhat over the interwar period. The most important was correspondence which rose modestly after a stable period between 1928 and 1932. Average postal rates declined to around 1½d or less from a peak of 1¾d between 1920 and 1922. Parcel traffic fluctuated rather more — there was a fall to 1922, a gradual increase to 1930, then a slow decline through to 1934–35, followed by a recovery to a new peak in 1938. Average parcel rates declined from a peak in 1920–22 to an average of 9d a parcel between 1924–34, and even lower rates in the later 1930s. After an initial decline remittance services rose rapidly, the increase being associated in part with pool betting.

The number of telephones installed rose steadily throughout the period. When the telephone system was nationalised in 1912 there were only 700,000 subscribers. By 1922 the one million mark was reached, then two million in 1932 and 3¼ million by 1939. The number of calls per telephone, however, declined steadily and by the end of the period the daily average was 1.8.

For the telegraph service, there was a gradual decline until 1935, when a recovery set in. The relative price of telegrams appears to have affected the variations. While retail prices on the whole were falling, telegram rates were almost stationary between 1925 and 1935. In addition to this, there were other factors operating to affect the demand for telegrams adversely, the most serious being the competition of the telephone.

TRANSPORT AND COMMUNICATIONS

Study Questions on Transport and Communications
(a) Why did motor transport grow so rapidly?
(b) Did the railways face unfair competition from road transport?
(c) Why was air transport unprofitable before 1939?

Recommended Reading on Transport and Communications
Aldcroft, D.H., *British Transport since 1914* (Newton Abbot, 1975)
Bagwell, P.S., *The Transport Revolution since 1770* (London, 1974)
Sturmey, S.G., *British Shipping and World Competition* (London, 1962)

9 The Distributive Trades

In terms of both output and employment the distributive trades were the fastest growing sector of services in the interwar period. Employment in distribution grew more rapidly than in any other sector and by the end of the period accounted for around 13 per cent of total employment compared with 10 per cent in 1920. However, distribution remained a labour-intensive occupation and, despite the growth of large-scale units in retailing, the productivity performance of the sector as a whole failed to improve.

The functions of the wholesaler were being telescoped in these years as some larger retail stores began to do their own wholesaling, while manufacturers cut out the wholesaler altogether by taking over many of his functions such as packaging and blending goods. Tentative estimates for 1938 suggest that 53 per cent of the total value of all retail sales originated direct from the producer or importer to the retailer, while 43 per cent passed through one or more wholesaling intermediaries and the remaining four per cent was done by producer-retailers. However, the loss of business to the wholesaler was probably not

THE DISTRIBUTIVE TRADES

very great. The importance of wholesaling varied a great deal from trade to trade and in some cases, for example fruit and vegetables, the functions of the wholesaler increased.

By far the largest branch of distribution was retailing and it was here that most of the growth occurred. Estimated retail sales in real terms rose by nearly 38 per cent between 1920 and 1938, and much of this increase in business went to the larger retailers. Before the First World War large units accounted for less than 20 per cent of all sales, but by 1939 they were responsible for one third or more of total trade and in some cases, such as footwear, women's clothing, groceries and provisions, dairy produce and chemist's goods, they accounted for more than 40 per cent of the total sales in each group.

There were three main types of large-scale retailers; the cooperative societies, the departmental stores and the multiples. Before the war the cooperatives, with about eight per cent of all retail business, had been the largest of the three groups. They continued to expand in the interwar years; membership of the movement increased from three million in 1914 to 6.5 million in 1938, though these figures give a somewhat inflated impression of the rate of development since they include many non-purchasing members. The main features of development were the spread of their activities into the Midlands and South, both areas having been neglected before the war, and an increase in the scale of operations both on the production and retailing sides. By 1939 the cooperatives accounted for around 10–11 per cent of all sales, but in view of their relatively strong pre-war position their progress in the retail field was disappointing. One reason for this may have been the concentration on a rather narrow range of staple products and a failure to branch out into those lines of activity where demand was expanding most rapidly. They were slow to develop modern methods of display and product quality did not improve very much. By the end of the period their main strength lay in food, household goods and clothing.

Departmental stores showed an increase from around three to four per cent of all sales to about five per cent but they were never a significant force in the retail market. Financial integration between stores developed rapidly and eventually four major groups controlled 200 or more stores. The absence of centralised control or direction from these groups meant that operating costs were relatively high, while fairly large outlays had to be made on advertising. On the whole departmental stores tended to concentrate heavily on women's and children's wear and drapery, though some expansion was registered in furniture, household goods, hardware, pottery and glass.

By far the most vigorous growth occurred in multiple-shop retailing. As a group it accounted for some six to seven per cent of all sales before the war, while the 1939 figure was around 18–19 per cent of retail trade, that is, a larger proportion than that of the cooperatives and departmental stores combined. Between 1910 and 1939 the number of separate branches (that is, of firms with 10 or more branches) more than doubled, from 19,852 to 44,487, while the number of firms rose from 395 to 680. Several changes took place in the structure and organisation of multiple retailing. The size of firms increased either by amalgamation or merger or by the opening of new branches. As a result some trades came to be dominated by one or two large groups, e.g. Freeman, Hardy and Willis in footwear, Home and Colonial Stores and the International Tea Group in groceries, Union Cold Storage in meat and in chemists' goods, Timothy White and Taylor, and Boots Pure Drug Company. But in most cases competition continued to prevail, since rarely was anything approaching a monopoly position gained by any one group. A further important development was the emergence of variety chain stores — their numbers quadrupled between 1920 and 1939 (300 to 1,200) and by the latter date they accounted for 20 per cent of the total sales by multiples, as against only three per cent in 1920. Some of the main groups in this sector included the well-known firms of Marks and Spencer, F.W. Woolworth, British Home Stores and Littlewoods.

Considerable changes also took place in the pattern of trading and the type of products sold by the multiples. In

Woolworths in the 1920s and 30s, typical of the variety chain stores which quadrupled in number between 1920 and 1939.

1915 just over 72 per cent of all sales was represented by food, a further 15 per cent consisted of clothing and the rest was divided among confectionery, stationery, tobacco and miscellaneous items. By the end of the period the system of trading catered much more for the varied demands, both as regards the goods offered and the range of services provided, of a wide section of the community. Food sales had declined to 45 per cent of the multiples' turnover, while clothing had increased to 26 per cent and other goods to 29 per cent. The multiples now sold a wide range of products including not only food and clothing, but also chemists' goods, pottery, glassware, hardware, jewellery, toys, sports goods, household equipment, books and furnishings. At the same time, in some of the more standardised commodities such as footwear, milk and chemists' goods, integration of the production and distribution processes had been carried out.

There were several factors responsible for the growth of large-scale units and the expansion in retailing generally. There were economies to be gained by selling and buying on a large scale and the development of new trading techniques made it possible to extend the scope of operations. Various factors, for example education and housing, helped to make the consumer market more homogeneous — people tended to buy similar things and this in turn widened the possibilities of national marketing and made possible the use of similar sales techniques by retailers in different parts of the country. This trend was reinforced by the spread of branded goods, the decline in the preparation of foods in the home, and the concomitant development of pre-packed goods, but, above all, by the rapid growth in the use of motor transport which not only increased the radius of the retailer's operations, but also affected the location of shops and the types of service offered. In addition, the increasing range of new household goods, especially consumer durables, also encouraged large-scale retailing, since many of these products were too expensive to be handled by small retailers.

During the Second World War the existing framework of the distributive trades remained practically intact.

THE DISTRIBUTIVE TRADES

Shortages of supplies, materials and capital meant that fewer people were distributing fewer goods, while methods and structure remained stable. The numbers employed in the distributive trades decreased by one third from 1938 to 1944, the resultant reduction in manpower causing additional consumer services to be cut. This was a period, however, when few developments in the structure and techniques of the distributive trades were made.

Study Questions on the Distributive Trades

(a) What contribution did the distributive trades make to the growth of employment?
(b) Explain the reasons for the growing importance of large-scale retailing.
(c) What changes took place in the pattern of retail trading?

Recommended Reading on the Distributive Trades

Jefferys, J.B., *Retail Trading in Britain, 1850–1950* (London, 1954)
Levy, H., *The Shops of Britain* (London, 1948)

10 Overseas Trade

Britain's position as an international trader was particularly important in this period since conditions changed so radically from those of the pre-1914 era, and these changes had important repercussions not only on Britain but also on the international economy as a whole. The central feature of the period was the declining importance of international trade in the British economy. In 1913 exports formed 23.2 per cent of net national income, while imports were somewhat higher at 31.1 per cent. By 1929 the relevant proportions were 17.6 and 26.7 per cent and by 1938 they had declined even further to 9.8 and 17.6 per cent respectively (measured in current values). The most disturbing aspect of the British trade position was the stagnation in exports. Before the war (1900–13) the volume of exports rose by 4.2 per cent per annum, whereas in the period 1920–38 they registered a negative rate of 1.2 per cent per annum and as high as –2.3 per cent over the years 1913–38. The volume of exports slumped sharply during the war and again in the trade recessions of 1921, 1929–32 and 1937–38, but in most of the intervening years they maintained a slow upward trend. However in no year did exports regain their 1913 level (see Table 14).

OVERSEAS TRADE

Table 14 Index Numbers of the Volume of Exports and Imports, 1919–38 (1913 = 100)

	Total exports	Coal exports	Total imports	Retained imports Total	Food	Materials	Fuel	Manufactures
1919	55.0	48.0	87.7					
1920	70.3	34.0	87.7	88.0	88.0	90.7	162.1	77.0
1921	49.5	33.6	74.1	73.5	90.8	55.2	210.5	50.5
1922	68.1	87.5	85.2	86.5	99.5	73.6	201.6	67.2
1923	74.7	108.3	92.6	96.9	114.7	73.0	218.6	83.3
1924	75.8	84.0	103.7	109.1	126.5	83.8	266.1	96.6
1925	74.7	69.2	107.4	113.1	124.3	90.3	262.9	109.8
1926	67.0	28.2	109.9	118.2	122.9	87.5	604.8	110.3
1927	76.9	69.7	112.3	121.2	127.5	91.5	380.7	123.6
1928	79.1	68.2	108.6	117.2	127.5	86.4	384.7	121.8
1929	81.3	82.1	114.8	124.2	131.8	96.3	391.9	127.6
1930	65.9	74.8	111.1	121.2	131.8	87.7	446.0	123.0
1931	50.5	58.2	113.6	124.2	143.6	82.1	418.6	126.4
1932	50.5	53.0	98.8	109.1	139.3	81.4	424.2	71.3
1933	51.6	53.2	98.8	111.1	135.0	90.7	466.9	69.0
1934	54.9	54.0	103.7	117.2	136.1	100.0	511.3	79.3
1935	59.3	52.7	104.9	118.2	135.0	101.9	529.8	82.8
1936	59.3	47.0	112.3	127.3	138.3	115.0	559.7	93.7
1937	64.8	55.0	118.5	134.3	139.3	126.2	583.9	105.2
1938	57.1	48.9	113.6	127.3	143.6	107.5	603.2	89.7

Sources: London and Cambridge Economic Service, *Key Statistics of the British Economy, 1900–1966*; B.R. Mitchell and P. Deane, *Abstract of British Historical Statistics* (Cambridge, 1962), pp. 121–2; M. Fg. Scott, *A Study of United Kingdom Imports* (Cambridge, 1963), pp. 244–5

There are a number of reasons for the long-term stagnation in Britain's exports. During the war Britain lost many markets because of her inability to supply goods and as a result countries formerly dependent on British goods either sought alternative sources of supply or began to produce the goods themselves. Recent studies suggest that the two most important influences affecting Britain's export position adversely were changes in the volume of world trade and competition, while losses due to changes in the area and commodity composition of trade were relatively modest. Britain's share of total world exports declined from 13.9 per cent in 1913 to 10.8 per cent in 1929 and 10.2 in 1937.

It could be argued that Britain's trade losses were greater than those of other countries because of adverse changes in patterns of demand relative to Britain's capacity to supply. For example, the industrialisation of new countries and the raising of tariffs led to import substitution on the part of former customers, while demand for some products, for example coal, was declining because of the development of substitutes. Similarly, the concentration of exports on markets of low income primary producers would tend to dampen down the growth of exports.

In these respects Britain was more vulnerable than most countries. A large proportion of exports in 1913 consisted of textiles, coal and basic engineering products such as railway materials and ships, all of which were declining sectors in world trade during this period. Furthermore, over 40 per cent of all exports went to primary producing countries, markets which were poor both from an income and import substitution point of view. The incomes of primary producing countries were depressed, especially in the 1930s, because of falling prices, while Britain was easily the principal loser from the process of import substitution in the semi-industrial countries. Over the period 1913–37 her losses in these markets were substantially greater than those of continental Western Europe and about four-fifths greater than those of the United States. The major losses through import substitution occurred in India and Latin America and the main product affected was textiles. In 1937 Britain's textile exports to India were only about one-seventh of the 1913 volume.

However, shifts in the pattern of economic relationships of a type unfavourable to Britain were not the only reason for her substantial losses. Evidence suggests that an additional factor was the deterioration in the ability of British industry to compete in world markets. In nearly every major industrial category, whether expanding, declining or stable from the point of view of world trade, Britain's share in each case declined, especially between 1913 and 1929. An index of export unit values (all manufactured exports) shows a value of 169 for the United Kingdom in 1929 (1913 = 100) compared with a weighted average of 134 for 12 major industrial countries. British export prices were higher relative to the prewar base than those of any other country and the price disadvantage affected all the main commodity groups.

Relatively speaking, Britain's ability to compete improved in the 1930s. Through the years 1929–37 British export prices ran fairly closely with those of other countries, though in the early 1930s the decline was more pronounced in Britain. This improvement can be attributed to a number of factors including the rather faster rate of growth in Britain in the 1930s and the initial gains from the depreciation of sterling in 1931. In addition, the system of Empire preference made trading conditions easier for Britain. On balance, however, Britain still remained competitively weak at the end of the period, since compared with 1913, export prices were higher than those of other countries.

Overall therefore competition was the main factor responsible for Britain's poor export performance in the interwar years. This was associated with the emergence of new competitors and new products, import substitution and a decline in Britain's ability to compete. In addition, unfavourable shifts in world demand relative to the composition of Britain's exports and the contraction in the volume of world trade in the 1930s were contributory factors.

In contrast to exports, imports remained above the prewar level for most of the period. They were at their lowest in the recession of 1921, but then rose steadily to a level of some 15 per cent above prewar by 1929. Imports remained on a plateau in the early years of the slump but then dropped sharply in 1932–33 after which they rose to a peak in 1937, when they exceeded the 1913 volume by 18.5 per cent (see Table 14). Generally speaking, imports, as exports, moved with the cycle.

There are several reasons why the volume of imports remained fairly buoyant. A large proportion of imports consisted of food, the demand for which was relatively inelastic with respect to price and income changes. The rising trend of imports was determined largely by the increase in population, though the rather abnormal price decline of imported foods may have led to some substitution between imported and home-produced foods, especially in the 1930s. The second main influence was the rapid rise in imported fuels. These increased in almost every year and reached a peak in 1938. About two-thirds of the fuel imports consisted of motor and aviation spirit which accounted for four-fifths of the increase in retained imports in this category between 1924 and 1938.

Though raw materials became relatively cheaper in this period, the volume of imports remained below the prewar level until the mid-1930s after which it rose sharply. Price changes no doubt had some effect on the level of imports, but this seems to have been more than offset by savings due to new techniques resulting in greater raw material economy, the substitution of new materials, the increasing use of scrap products and a shift in the pattern of output towards industries with a lower average raw material content or with less reliance on imported supplies.

Compared with other major groups, the demand for imported manufactured goods was much more elastic with respect to price and income changes, while imported products were often fairly close substitutes with those manufactured in Britain. Thus it is not surprising to find that imports rose fairly rapidly in the later 1920s and between 1935–37, when domestic activity and incomes were particularly buoyant. On the other hand, imports of manufactures rose continuously throughout the 1920s which suggests that cheaper foreign goods were being substituted for domestic production. Manufactured imports remained at a high level in 1930 and 1931, and in the latter year at least this was probably due to stockpiling in order to beat the tariff.

The very sharp drop in the volume of imports in 1931–33, by no less than 45 per cent, can be attributed to the tariff rather than to changes in domestic incomes or the price effects of devaluation. The fall in income was very modest in 1931–32 and it was more than offset by a sharp rise in the following year, while the price of imported manufactures in terms of sterling (excluding the tariff) actually fell. Since imports respond largely to changes in the level of domestic activity it was only to be expected that, with rising real incomes and population, the volume of imports would be greater than in 1913. No doubt at times imports of manufactures might appear unduly large, but the overall import trend was not excessive compared with changes in domestic activity. In fact, in relation to income trends, import growth was substantially lower than before the war, especially in the 1930s. Moreover, the ratio of the percentage growth of the import volume to that of GNP was around 0.6 for the period 1924–37, compared with an average ratio of 0.5 for Western Europe and 1.5 for the United States and Canada. Thus from the payments point of view (though here we are speaking without reference to prices and values) the problem was not the unusually high level of imports, but rather the failure of exports to expand to meet the importing propensity of a growing economy.

During the 1939–45 period, home industry was to be increasingly diverted to war production and therefore maintenance of the peacetime level of exports could not be expected. On the other hand, imports, though controlled, were likely to hold up rather better because of the need for essential supplies. Exports were switched from areas with the 'hardest' currencies to those with vital strategic materials to sell in return. By doing so, many traditional markets were lost and the volume of exports fell to less than a third of the prewar figure. Before the war 9.5 per cent of the labour force had been engaged on exports, but by 1945 this figure had declined to less than two per cent.

Study Questions on Overseas Trade

(a) Explain the collapse of British exports after 1920.
(b) Were British exports uncompetitive in the interwar years?

(c) What factors determined the trend in imports during the period?

Recommended Reading on Overseas Trade

Booker, H.S., *The Problem of Britain's Overseas Trade* (London, 1948)

Kindleberger, C.P., 'Foreign Trade and Growth: Lessons from British Experience since 1913', *Lloyds Bank Review*, 65 (1962)

Maizels, A., *Industrial Growth and World Trade* (Cambridge, 1963)

Scott, M. Fg., *A Study of United Kingdom Imports* (Cambridge, 1963)

11 The Balance of Payments

It is difficult to make precise generalisations about movements in the balance of payments during this period, since the main components of the external account changed in different ways. Moreover, the statistics for this period leave much to be desired, though recent work has done much to improve their presentation.[1]

Throughout the period the current balance moved steadily from surplus to deficit. In 1920 a positive balance of £315 million was recorded, but by 1938 this had been transformed into a deficit of £65 million. This was due to unfavourable trends both in the trade balance and the invisible account. The deterioration in the trade balance was to be expected given the unfavourable relationship between the volume of exports and imports, though in part this was offset by an improvement in the terms on

---

1. Much of this section is based on the revised estimates for interwar balance of payments figures prepared by R.G. Ware, 'The Balance of Payments in the Interwar Period: Further Details' *Bank of England Quarterly Bulletin*, 14 (March 1974), pp. 47–52.

which goods were exchanged. Over the period 1913–38 the net barter terms of trade (the ratio between the price of exports and imports) improved by 43 per cent though the improvement was somewhat less for the years 1920–38. It was also unevenly distributed over time, most of it occurring in 1921 and again between 1929 and 1933. This meant that for the periods 1920–29 and 1930–38 the average deficit on the trade balance deteriorated less than might have been expected, from £205 million to £256 million.

Before the war and for a time afterwards, Britain's trade deficit was more than covered by a large surplus on invisibles, which meant that there was a good positive balance for investment overseas. Unfortunately, the strength of the invisible account weakened considerably during the course of the interwar period. Receipts in the form of dividends, interest etc. declined partly because of the general decline in profitability of such investments especially in the 1930s. Default on investments and curtailed foreign lending also made for lower earnings. In addition, shipping earnings and income derived by financial institutions for services rendered to foreigners declined in importance, especially during the world depression of the 1930s. The upshot of these adverse trends was that the annual surplus on invisible account declined from £319 million in the 1920s to £216 million in the following decade. Not surprisingly therefore, the overall current account shifted from an annual surplus of some £114 million in the 1920s to a deficit of £40 million on average in the 1930s.

The consequence of the deterioration in the current account was a sharply reduced flow of investment overseas. The average outflow in the first period was about £115 million per annum, but by the 1930s it had shrunk to a mere £15 million. The primary cause of this decline was undoubtedly the fact that the surplus on current account was insufficient to support a volume of lending of prewar dimensions. However, it should also be noted that international economic conditions were much less favourable for large-scale overseas investment than before 1914. This was especially true in the 1930s when new overseas issues raised in London declined sharply partly as a result of various embargoes, while at the same time repayments on existing loans increased. Indeed, in the period 1935–38 more money entered London on loan acount than flowed out.

Thus by 1938 Britain's balance of payments was in a very much weaker position than it had been before the war, or for that matter in the early 1920s. There was a larger deficit on visible trade transactions which was only partly covered by the reduced earnings on the invisible account, and this resulted in an overall deficit on current account. A summary of the changes in the balance of payments position is provided in Table 15.

Table 15 Balance of Payments of the UK 1920–38 (£m. annual averages)

	1920–29	1930–38
Visible balance	−205	−256
Invisible balance	+319	+216
Current balance	+114	−40
Identified capital movements	−115	−15
Balancing item[a]	+9	+87
Currency flow	+8	+32
Visible deficit as a percentage of GNP	4.1	5.2
Current surplus or deficit as a percentage of GNP	2.3	0.8

Note: (a) Before 1928 this includes changes in short-term liabilities and acceptances.

Source: R.G. Ware, 'The Balance of Payments in the Interwar Period: Further Details', *Bank of England Quarterly Review*, 14 (March 1974), p. 47

Study Questions on the Balance of Payments

(a) Why did Britain's balance of payments deteriorate in the interwar years?
(b) Why did capital exports dwindle in the 1930s?
(c) How did Britain gain from movements in the terms of trade?

Recommended Reading on the Balance of Payments

Royal Institute of International Affairs, *The Problem of International Investment* (London, 1937)

Ware, R.G., 'The Balance of Payments in the Interwar Period' *Bank of England Quarterly Bulletin,* 14 (March 1974)

12 Financial Institutions

Between 1920 and 1945 the total assets of Britain's financial institutions rose from £4.6 billion to £15.8 billion. Over the same period:
   (a) bank and discount companies'[1] assets increased from £2.7 to £6.5 billion;
   (b) building societies' increased from £87 to £824 million;
   (c) insurance companies' increased from £0.7 to £2.4 billion;
   (d) the Post Office Savings Bank's rose from £267 to nearly £1,800 million; and
   (e) trustee savings banks' rose from £94 to £619 million.

These figures reflect a sizable rise in the pace of financial activity. However, relative growth rates differed considerably, and the changing structure in each group's share of all institutional assets can be seen in Table 16. The bank

---

1. Discount companies, or houses, were originally (and as used here) financial firms who lent to the government by holding short-dated government paper including Treasury bills, and to the private sector by holding commercial bills.

Table 16 Total Assets of Financial Institutions and Percentage Share Attributable to Each Component 1920–45

Percentage Contribution to Total Financial Institutions' Assets of Particular Intermediaries

Year	Total Financial Assets (£m.)	Banks and Discount Companies	Life Insurance Companies	Post Office Savings Bank	Building Societies	Trustee Savings Banks	National Savings Bonds	Friendly Societies	Hire-Purchase Societies
1920	4,552	59.5	16.4	5.9	1.9	2.1	11.6	2.6	–
1930	5,799	47.8	22.3	5.0	6.4	2.4	11.9	3.9	0.1
1939	8,126	41.3	23.2	6.8	9.5	3.2	10.3	5.0	0.2
1945	15,779	40.7	15.0	11.3	5.2	3.9	19.6	3.7	0.1

Source: D.K. Sheppard, *The Growth and Role of U.K. Financial Institutions 1880–1962* (London, 1971), p. 3

and discount companies' share steadily declined from 59.5 per cent in 1920 to 40.7 per cent in 1945, while the building societies' share rose from 1.9 per cent to a peak of 9.9 per cent in 1938 and then declined to 5.2 per cent in 1945.

In the peacetime period the building societies did well, while the assets of the banks and the Post Office Savings Bank either expanded slowly or declined. In contrast, wartime meant prosperity for the banks and the Post Office Savings Bank and decline or slower growth for building societies and trustee savings banks.

World War I necessitated and expedited a larger degree of government involvement in finance. High interest-yielding savings certificates were issued in 1916 through the National Savings scheme. This proved to be very successful not only in World War I but also in World War II when the National Savings Bonds' share of the market rose substantially to 19.6 per cent (see Table 16).

Government committees played important roles in postwar financial policies. For example, on the advice of the Cunliffe Committee, which reported in 1918–19, the government decided to return to gold, which necessitated bringing prices down into line with those of the United States, something which could only be brought about by severe credit restriction. In the export field, the British Trade Corporation was established as a result of the guidelines set out by the Farrington Committee of 1916. In this way export finance was stimulated in order to correct the balance of payments position.

The government also sought to channel funds to credit-needy sectors. The Housing and Town Planning Act of 1919 provided for low-interest loans to stimulate low-cost housing. Through the passage of the Agricultural Credits Acts of 1923 and 1928, the state tried to boost this declining industry. The United Dominion Trust was formed in 1920 in order to bolster hire-purchase finance.

In addition to this fund-channelling, a government directive issued in 1918 caused the banks to stop further amalgamation, and in 1920 the banks agreed to limit their advances so that the government's deflationary policy could be carried out more effectively.

The Balfour, Macmillan and Enfield Committees' reports had decisive influences on government financial policy in the thirties. The Macmillan Committee in particular played an important role — its aim was to 'inquire into banking, finance and credit ... and to make recommendations calculated to enable these agencies to promote the development of trade and commerce and the employment of labour'.[2]

By 1932 the path was set for state financial management — the gold standard was abandoned in 1931, the Exchange Equalisation Account and the concept of the sterling area were established and the UK capital market was closed to non-sterling area issues. By 1939 the government had made sure that no privately-controlled savings movement could have any serious repercussions on the rate of government borrowing without the government's prior permission.

The state's role became increasingly important as it acquired and exercised more powers to regulate the development of financial institutions. For example, the growth of the building societies was undoubtedly stimulated by the state's aid to the housing industry. At the same time, the increasing number of social service benefits retarded

---

2. *Report of the Committee on Finance and Industry*, Cmd. 389 (HMSO, 1931), p. 1.

The General Strike, fifth day, 8 May 1926. An armoured car escorting food-convoys through Oxford Circus en route to Hyde Park for distribution.

the growth of the insurance companies.

The institutions' response to state management was to be far from passive; in fact, pressure groups in the form of trade associations to represent their interests were set up. There was an increasing tendency towards cartelisation. Common interest-rates in institutions not subject to state regulation were established; guidelines were set out as to the nature of business in which the institutions should engage. By 1931 the banks had shown a definite similarity in their patterns of distribution of assets. This was also true of insurance companies, building societies, trustee savings banks and the Post Office Savings Bank. This adherence to a conventional pattern, that is, a growing cartelisation, led to certain inflexibilities, such as a deficiency in the conversion process of financial savings into medium-term loans. Banks set up barriers by restricting, for example, the provision of clearing services which would benefit financial competitors.

The increasingly oligopolistic tendency meant that entry into the market could be restricted; not only the banks but also other institutions exerted restraining pressures on new entrants. As a result of this cartelisation, gaps in the financial framework developed. The Bank of England and the government made attempts to fill these gaps. The Bank appointed development authorities to help credit-needy sectors, for example, agriculture, and the government helped to eliminate unsatisfied demands for housing finance by directly subsidising local authority and private low-cost housing projects. State and Bank intervention in turn boosted confidence in the institutions they assisted; growth in the business of hire-purchase companies, for example, was very rapid during the years 1920–36.

At the same time, government statutory regulations tended to fix the financial market structure even more firmly and the practices of the institutions tended to reinforce this tendency. The special relationships between the individual groups were maintained, and adventurous financial innovations were discouraged. For example, the building societies played an increasingly important part in the funding of bank construction loans and in turn the banks provided them with short-term financial accommodation. Also the banks provided more and more finance to the hire-purchase companies; by 1930 bank financial accommodation accounted for nearly 40 per cent of their resources.

As financial groups sought to minimise the extent of interest rate competition, so the tendency towards a fixed financial structure with respect to the type and term of borrowings and savings became even more pronounced. Moreover, the mutual benefits of market-sharing arrangements were well recognised.

In addition, the decline in the relative importance of Britain as an economic power in the international economy necessitated adaptation on the part of financial institutions and government policy towards finance. There was a marked reduction in bank holdings of commercial bills[3] as a result of wartime demands — between 1914 and 1920 the share of commercial bills in bank holdings of bills discounted fell from 95 to 59 per cent; it declined further to 41 per cent in 1938 and to as little as 15 per cent by the end of the Second World War. Thus the UK's potential contribution to the supply of short-term international loans was reduced. During the early 1930s the merchant banks were adversely affected by the decline in international trade and lending, and they would have been in grave difficulties had the Bank of England not stepped in and saved them by rediscount facilities.[4] The impediments to trade, the spread of tariff barriers, the rapid growth in the economic power of Britain's trading rivals, and two major wars radically changed the country's financial position.

---

3. A written instruction by the person drawing it (the drawer) to another (the drawee) to pay a particular sum either to the bearer of the bill, or to the order of a specified person (the payee).

4. The discounting of something which has already changed hands at a discount; a term largely used with reference to dealings in commercial and Treasury bills.

FINANCIAL INSTITUTIONS

Study Questions on Financial Institutions

(a) Account for the growth of building societies in the period.
(b) How did the relative importance of various financial institutions change between 1920 and 1939?
(c) What effect did state policy have on financial institutions?

Recommended Reading on Financial Institutions

Balogh, T., *Studies in Financial Organization* (Cambridge, 1947)
Grant, A.T.K., *A Study of the Capital Market in Britain from 1919 to 1936* (London, 1967)
Sheppard, D.K., *The Growth and Role of U.K. Financial Institutions 1880–1962* (London, 1971)

13 Currency and Credit

The First World War shattered the basis of the gold standard order, despite the fact that it remained intact in its external forms. Initially there was a complete breakdown of international financial markets and sterling rose to well above $5.00 on the foreign exchanges, as London ceased new foreign undertakings and finished with the old; with increased shipping risks, and later the authorities' refusal to include gold under the war risks insurance scheme, the gold points[1] became irrelevant as far as shipping gold was concerned. The sterling exchange returned to more normal levels when the authorities agreed to pay sterling for gold deposited in Ottawa. However, as more and more resources were going to the war effort and as British prices and demand for American goods rose while exports declined, sterling soon fell below the prewar gold export

---

1. Gold points or gold specie points were the limits within which an exchange rate of a country on the gold standard was likely to deviate before it became profitable to ship gold in or out of the country. These limits were known as the gold export or import points; hence at the gold export point it would become profitable to export gold and *vice versa*.

point[2] on the dollar exchange. At the same time there was a depreciation of the major allied currencies against sterling. During 1915 the exchanges became pegged by official borrowing and intervention with the proceeds. The intervention peg[3] for the dollar exchange was $4.76⁷⁄₁₆. At about the same time, the Allies' exchanges were also pegged near the prewar gold pars and it was behind this framework that international cost and price levels diverged substantially under the impact of war. By this time it was clear that the problem of Britain's future exchange policy necessitated a solution.

In an attempt to find a solution a number of committees, such as the Cunliffe Committee of 1918, were appointed, the main task being to provide information on how best to bring back a state of normal conditions. Eventually, as the cost of pegging became very high, in March 1919 official support ceased for the sterling-dollar exchange, which resulted in a sharp fall in the exchange rate. The Bank of England was very slow to deal with this situation and the Bank Rate was not raised to 6 per cent until November 1919, and then to 7 per cent early in 1920, when the postwar boom was about to break. This action had obviously come too late; however, the Bank was in a difficult position since it had little effective control over the market due to the high liquidity of the commercial banks and business firms, and the existence of a large floating debt. In fact, in the first half of 1919, the Treasury not the Bank was the real arbiter of market conditions, and raising the Bank Rate increased the cost of debt operations. Not only this, but if the rate differential between commercial bills[4] and Treasury bills[5] was widened, there was the danger that the Treasury bills coming up for renewal might not be taken

---

2. See note 1.
3. Artificial fixing of a country's exchange rate at a certain 'pegged' level — usually practised in wartime.
4. See Chapter 12, note 3.
5. A document by which the British government borrows money for a short period of time.

up. This would force the government to borrow on Ways and Means[6] from the Bank, resulting in additional funds in the market, thereby offsetting the credit contraction brought about by the initial rise in interest rates.

The downswing was not only aggravated by the bad timing of the Bank's policy, but also by the deflationary budget of 1920 and the Treasury's decision to limit the note issue. This restrictive policy was maintained until well into 1922. By the latter date however the Bank of England had regained control of financial markets. As the Bank made use of open market operations in Treasury bills and also made use of new contracts with market institutions formed during wartime operations, it meant that the Bank's operational position was potentially much stronger than it had been in the prewar period. The Bank then began to use this new power by participating in open market operations designed to reduce the assets of the market. Even so, given the domestic situation the Bank's policy was hardly appropriate. This could be explained in part by the weakness of the foreign exchanges; also adherence to relatively high interest rates reflected the Bank's desire to prevent losing control over the market as had happened in 1919, and at the same time to ensure that the market would absorb the large volume of Treasury bills and relieve the government as much as possible from resorting to Ways and Means borrowing.

At the end of 1922 the authorities were in a position to consider tactics for a return to par. But for over a year, from mid-1922, priority was given to domestic considerations. This can be seen in the series of Bank Rate reductions to 3 per cent, and the mid-1922 open market operations which caused the market's indebtedness to the Bank to fall and the Bank's holdings of government securities to rise. A year of easy money followed.

---

6. These are part of the floating debt — they represent day-to-day (overnight) interest-free lending to the Exchequer by the Bank of England from surplus balances on internal account of government departments and extra-budgetary funds, e.g. national insurance funds.

CURRENCY AND CREDIT

The Bank's position had been considerably eased by the strengthening of the exchanges in 1922–23 — in February 1923, the sterling-dollar exchange rose to a peak of $4.72. It was about this time that the question of returning to the gold standard came to exercise a greater influence over the Bank's policy. The floating exchange system of the early 1920s proved that the sterling-dollar rate was below the prewar level, so that artificial forcing up would be necessary to reach the former rate of $4.86. Despite this realisation, the exchanges were strong enough to maintain a 4 per cent Bank Rate throughout 1924 and it was not until March 1925 that it was raised to 5 per cent in order to bring funds in from abroad to get the rate back to parity.

In April 1925 Britain returned to the gold standard at the prewar parity of $4.86. This was at a time when unemployment stood at 11 per cent, there were substantial capital losses in industry, and when British exports remained below the prewar level. Keynes was one of the most ardent critics of the return — he argued that at the old parity the pound would be overvalued by 10 per cent. This was in fact borne out by the internal price levels; even at a favourable time, April 1925, British internal prices were 176 compared with 165 in the USA. After 1925 world prices fell and several countries, including France, Belgium and Germany, returned to gold at lower parities, thus aggravating Britain's competitive handicap. The City thought that its prosperity, regardless of the cost to other sectors of the economy, was paramount and would benefit the economy as a whole. It was essentially a City decision to return, not a decision of the industrialists.

The consequences of returning at too high a level were serious. A 10 per cent price differential handicapped export industries at a time when Britain was already falling behind most other industrial countries. The maintenance of high interest rates kept up the burdens of the national debt charge and thus of taxation; they burdened business with many fixed payments at unnecessarily high rates; they attracted unstable funds from abroad. Thus dear money had the effect of preserving foreign exchanges, but partly at the expense of employment and domestic activity.

Changes in the banking structure and the money market interfered with the automatic regulative function of the Bank of England's gold reserve. High interest rates attracted short-term foreign funds which left as soon as the rates went down. Before the war London had been the chief credit centre, and it forced its monetary policies onto the rest of the world, but afterwards there were two or possibly three centres, London, New York and Paris. This division of authority, together with London's declining power, served to complicate the process of maintaining international monetary equilibrium. The effectiveness of monetary control by London was also altered by the large number of Treasury bills outstanding.

Even at the best of times it would have been difficult for the gold standard to function efficiently in view of the structural changes. Added to the internal problems was an unfavourable international position and by the end of the 1920s the harm that British monetary policy had caused was well understood. When the New York stock exchange boom collapsed there was a flow of gold to London and the Bank Rate was reduced. Eventually, however, Britain was affected by the downward trend of world prices — prices, production and employment all turned down sharply. 1931 saw the greatest international financial crisis ever known. Great strains were put on banks by falling prices. The collapse of the Austrian Kredit-Anstalt produced widespread loss of confidence in European finance, reduced international banking liquidity and subsequently many countries, unable to realise assets held abroad, were forced to freeze their own foreign indebtedness. Germany was at the centre of the crisis and the Reichsbank was in such a weak position that it needed help, in part provided by the Bank of England. To balance the withdrawal of foreign short-term funds, the Bank of England's gold reserve was allowed to fall to £130 million, since its second line of reserve, bill portfolios,[7] was frozen by moratoria.

---

7. The composition of a portfolio of bills, that is, the proportion of different types of bills in any one holding; as with a share portfolio made up of the stocks of different companies.

CURRENCY AND CREDIT

Bank Rate was raised to 4½ per cent, but the drain continued and loans raised in Paris and New York in the summer of 1931 prevented the Bank Rate from being driven up any further, but failed to save the gold standard.

The desire to end the strain on the internal economy by abandoning gold paved the way for lower interest rates. By April 1932 the pound was stabilised, the budget was balanced and the crisis was over. By June the Bank Rate had been reduced to 2 per cent. Cheap money was accompanied by a period of stable prices, interest rates and exchange rates. In April 1932 the Exchange Equalisation Account was established, the primary aim of which was to reduce or eliminate temporary fluctuations in the sterling exchange rate and to insulate the internal economy from the effects of capital and gold flows. The EEA began when sterling was in a relatively strong position and therefore quickly acquired large amounts of foreign currency in exchange for sterling bills. The Account operated in such a way as to prevent foreign capital movements from influencing the domestic credit structure. Also, it was to counteract any temporary divergence from the stabilised exchange rates by suitable purchases and sales, so that Britain could fix whatever was considered to be the desirable rates of sterling to any currency linked to gold.

Initially however, the EEA had a difficult task. It did not have much gold or holdings of foreign currencies with a fixed gold equivalent with which to purchase sterling. But in 1933 when the United States' banking system collapsed and Holland, Belgium and Switzerland ran into troubles, Britain was suddenly viewed as the safest haven for funds. The Account then possessed the resources to buy and sell sterling effectively.

Money continued to be cheap — Bank Rate remained at 2 per cent from 1932 to 1939 and bill rates stayed at around ½ per cent until 1939. The government pursued this policy for various reasons. Low rates in London would keep away foreign 'hot' money; they also kept government expenditure down without causing social unrest; and they helped encourage domestic investment and boosted investors' confidence. On the other hand, during the 1930s there was a gradual decline in the supply of Treasury bills, which made the banks less liquid and bank credit contracted, thereby partly offsetting the expansionary effect of cheap money.

It is difficult to give any precise estimates or conclusions as to the effect of cheap money on recovery in the 1930s. It cannot be regarded as crucial, since there were many other favourable aspects operating, for example, devaluation, tariff protection, a shift in the terms of trade, improved confidence as well as natural forces. Cheap money was perhaps least effective in terms of bank lending to industry and most influential in the housing market. Recovery would no doubt have been less vigorous had cheaper credit not been available.

After seven years of a 2 per cent Bank Rate it was raised to 4 per cent in 1939, but soon went down to 2 per cent, a level at which it stayed for the duration of the Second World War; hence the authorities were able to soak up all the available savings at low and steady rates. Any funds not invested in either the National Savings Scheme or National War Bonds went into the banks — these funds were in turn absorbed by Ways and Means Advances, Treasury bills and Treasury Deposit Receipts.[8]

A probable adverse balance of payments position during the war posed a threat to the value of sterling. Imports were likely to remain the same as in peacetime while exports could be expected to shrink. Invasion and the consequent need for war production forced Britain to sacrifice its exports and its gold and dollar reserve. 'Lend-lease' (American financial and economic aid in the Second World War) solved the dollar import problem and it became possible to switch exports to areas with vital strategic materials to sell in return. By doing so the volume of exports fell to less than one-third of the prewar figure and many traditional markets were lost.

Import controls and financial controls were used to keep the pound at a fixed value of $4.03. The Treasury control-

---

8. A form of compulsory lending by British banks to the Exchequer in the Second World War.

led all dealings in gold and foreign exchange; Treasury sanction was necessary for payments abroad and foreign asset purchases. However, these controls left some loopholes, for example, foreign holders of sterling balances could still participate in exchange dealings, and often sterling was exchanged for dollars or other 'hard' currency, which then escaped control.

Study Questions on Currency and Credit

(a) What factors determined monetary policy in the 1920s?
(b) Did the restored gold standard of 1925–31 benefit or retard Britain's economy?
(c) Discuss the role of cheap money in the recovery of the 1930s.

Recommended Reading on Currency and Credit

Aldcroft, D.H., 'The Impact of British Monetary Policy, 1919–1939', *International Review of the History of Banking*, 3 (1970)

Howson, S., *Domestic Monetary Management, 1919–1938* (Cambridge, 1976)

Nevin, E., *The Mechanism of Cheap Money: A Study of British Monetary Policy, 1931–1939* (Cardiff, 1955)

Pollard, S. (ed.), *The Gold Standard and Employment Policies between the Wars* (London, 1970)

Williams, D., 'London and the 1931 Financial Crisis', *Economic History Review*, 15 (1962–63)

14 Public Finance

Before 1914 the state tended to confine its activities to a narrow range of functions which principally included the regulation of economic enterprise (for example the Factory Acts and legislation to control the railways) in order to safeguard the consumer and employee, together with the expenditure of relatively small amounts of money on law enforcement, defence of the realm and certain social services. Consequently the state's instruments of control were both limited and weak. It owned or controlled directly very little and the volume of government expenditure was generally too small for variations in it to exert a substantial effect on the level of economic activity, even had there been any disposition to use expenditure for this purpose.

During the war the government became a 'giant practitioner' in industry. Eventually most forms of economic activity were controlled in some way or other and by 1918 two-thirds, or possible more, of all employed workers were engaged in activities subject to government control. Although most of the controls were quickly dismantled after hostilities, the wartime system of economic administration provided the government with considerable experience in economic matters and there were a few legacies for the future.

The second and perhaps most important effect of the war was the boost it gave to public expenditure. By 1918 total government expenditure (both central and local) accounted for over one half of GNP compared with only 13 per cent in 1913. The level of expenditure dropped sharply once military operations ceased, but the proportion of income dispensed by the state never returned to the prewar level. The war, by raising ideas as to the tolerable level of taxation and by revealing some of the glaring gaps in welfare provisions, caused a permanent displacement effect in total spending. It is true that over the interwar period there was no marked tendency for the relative importance of state expenditure to increase, but the level of that expenditure was much higher than prewar, ranging from between 24 and 30 per cent of GNP. Given the importance of the public sector it was perfectly possible to manipulate expenditure in a way which would help to counter economic fluctuations.

The interwar years presented an ideal opportunity for experimenting with fiscal policy. High and fluctuating levels of unemployment provided the need for a new approach, while the government's large claim over resources provided the means to manipulate aggregate demand. Taking the period as a whole, government expenditure in monetary terms showed no tendency to rise, though in real terms there was a substantial absolute increase. Local government spending tended to rise slightly faster than central expenditure and on average it accounted for over one-third of total public expenditure, though this was a lower proportion than before the war. On the other hand, local authorities accounted for the bulk of the capital expenditure since the Central Government had few powers to raise finance for investment purposes. For the period as a whole public and semi-public investment formed about 40 per cent of the total, and if housing is excluded the share is somewhat higher, reaching a peak of 50 per cent in the early 1930s. Clearly a claim on investment resources of this magnitude was a potentially powerful weapon in pursuing a counter-cyclical fiscal policy.

There were some notable changes in the pattern of public expenditure and taxation structure in the years after 1914. Before the war the bulk of government expenditure went on the purchases of goods and services and 20 per cent or less was paid out in transfers and subsidies. By 1920 the latter accounted for 38 per cent of total spending and with the heavy increase in transfer payments as a result of unemployment this proportion rose to 50 per cent and remained at this level until the later 1930s. The relative importance of different categories of expenditure also changed quite markedly. In 1913 military defence, social services and economic services accounted for 29.9, 33.0 and 12.9 per cent respectively of total expenditure. By 1918 military spending absorbed four-fifths of the total and even in 1920 it still accounted for nearly one-third. The proportion going to social services had dropped to 25.9 per cent, while servicing the national debt took 20.4 per cent of all spending. After reaching a peak of 29.7 per cent in 1924, the share taken by the national debt declined steadily to 13.4 per cent in 1938. The importance of military expenditure declined until the mid-1930s while social expenditure increased, so that in 1934 they accounted for 11.2 and 47.0 per cent respectively. Thereafter the trends were reversed as military expenditure rose and by 1938 the corresponding shares were 29.8 and 37.6 per cent respectively.

Changes in the tax structure were not as great as one might have expected. In 1913–14 five sources contributed 85 per cent of the Central Government's revenue; they were income and surtax[1] (27 per cent), estate duties (16), alcohol (25), tobacco (11) and tea and sugar (6). By the middle of the 1920s these five items still produced 80 per cent of the revenue, though there had been a significant shift in the relative importance of each one. Income and surtax now provided 43 per cent of the total, while the shares of the other four categories had fallen.

---

1. A special rate on incomes above a certain figure.

Occasionally in the interwar years budget deficits were recorded, notably in the immediate postwar years and again in 1932–33. Wartime fiscal policy had been highly inflationary and by 1917–18 the internal deficit of the Central Government amounted to about 40 per cent of net national income. Government spending was at an all time high and the budget deficit for 1918–19 amounted to £1,690 million. By the spring of 1919 conditions were such as to call for a policy of fiscal retrenchment (that is, fiscal tightening, or a cutting back on public outlays). Yet little was done to check the boom. Central Government expenditure, though lower than that of the year before, continued at a high level in 1919–20 and a budget deficit of £326.2 million was recorded for that year. Local government spending actually increased and the combined budgets of the local authorities ran into deficit, about the only time this happened in the period.

It was not until the boom was just about to break that the government decided to deflate. The Budget of 1920 raised taxes and this resulted in a substantial budget surplus for the year. Deflationary budgetary policies were pursued in the next two or three years in an effort to achieve a surplus to pay off the national debt and to pave the way for the return to the gold standard. Though certain taxes were reduced, these measures were too late, and in any case government expenditure was sharply reduced. There is little doubt, therefore, that budgetary policy intensified the downswing of 1921 and delayed the subsequent recovery. However, total government expenditure (in real terms) fell only very slightly in 1921 and 1922 and as a proportion of GNP it was higher than in 1920. This was due mainly to the high level of local authority spending.

In 1924 Snowden attempted to reverse the deflationary policy and this was continued by successive Chancellors for much of the 1920s. Some indirect taxes were reduced, the income tax was cut by 6d in the pound in 1925, most enterprises secured rate relief in 1929, while there was a substantial increase in social welfare expenditure. Most of these items were covered by increasing tax yields or by revenue from new imposts (new levies or duties) so that the budget remained more or less balanced. Fiscal policy was not entirely neutral however. Expenditure of both central and local authorities rose in the later 1920s, though as a proportion of GNP it remained fairly stable. On balance therefore, budgetary policy was probably mildly expansionary rather than neutral.

Fiscal policy was not adapted to meet the needs of the 1929–32 slump; in fact rather the reverse. In 1930 income tax and the duties on beer and petrol were raised, while during the economy campaign of 1931, both indirect and direct taxes were raised and so were unemployment contributions. To contain expenditure the salaries of public employees, including teachers and civil servants, were cut, transfer benefits were reduced and reductions were made in appropriations to the sinking fund.[2]

Despite these severe measures the full effect was not felt until 1932–33, so that total government spending in real terms continued to rise throughout the depression, and as a proportion of GNP it rose from 24 per cent in 1929 to a peak of 29 per cent in 1931 and then fell back slightly in the following year. Thus government expenditure exerted a mildly stabilising effect during the depression.

For nearly two years after the depression little was done to relax the economy measures and in 1932–34 spending by all public authorities fell quite sharply. Finally, in the budget of 1934, the standard rate of income tax was reduced by 6d (to 4s 6d), unemployment rates were restored and half the cuts in government salaries, the other half being made good the following year. Under the influence of military preparations expenditure rose very rapidly in the later 1930s; between 1935 and 1938 total government expenditure rose by more than £200 million in real terms with over half the increase occurring in 1938. At that date defence expenditure accounted for 30 per cent of the total compared to 11 per cent in 1935. Because of re-

---

2. A fund into which sums are placed periodically in order that they and the accrued interest may eventually pay off a debt, or be used to replace an asset. In this context the appropriations are towards repaying the National Debt.

armament government expenditure reached a peak in the recession of 1938.

Turning to the main items of government spending we find that the stabilising or destabilising effects of each one varied somewhat over different phases of the cycle. At the end of the First World War direct government expenditure on goods and services was running at a very high level, accounting for something like 45 per cent of GNP and 62 per cent of all public spending. Once the war had ended this expenditure fell sharply, especially between 1919 and 1920, so that it helped to moderate the boom. It continued to fall steadily through to 1923 and thereafter rose slowly and levelled out in the later 1920s, when on average it was slightly lower than in the two years 1921–22. In the subsequent slump it followed a counter-cyclical course through to 1931 but then fell back in the last year of recession. During the next two years it remained on a plateau and hence did little to assist initial recovery. After 1934 it rose steadily and accelerated rapidly in the later 1930s when it came to be dominated by armament expenditure. In 1937 and 1938 it amounted to 15 and 20 per cent of GNP as against 16 per cent in 1920.

Public investment followed a more clearly defined counter-cyclical course. In 1921, for example, public and semi-public investment rose very sharply at a time when private investment was beginning to tail off. During the next two years it declined, and after 1923 rose steadily but levelled out at the top of the boom in the later 1920s. It then rose again in the depression years of 1930 and 1931. In the two most critical years, 1932 and 1933, public investment was cut back, though in 1933 this was compensated by a large upswing in private investment. Thereafter both public and private investment increased through to 1938.

The main items of expenditure in public investment were those on dwellings, electricity supply, highways and bridges, social and public services, railways and postal and telecommunications. In the recession of 1921 nearly all of them increased, though in the following year, before recovery was properly under way, expenditure in most cases fell, the main exception being expenditure on roads

A typical modern kitchen of the 1930s from the 1935 Royal Academy exhibition of British Art in Industry. By the late 1930s, two out of every three houses were wired for electricity, as against one in seventeen in 1920.

which rose steadily until 1925. On the other hand, in the early 1930s there were much wider variations. Residential investment remained fairly stable to 1931 and then declined. Capital expenditure by the GPO followed a similar course, while railway investment was well maintained until a year later and then fell sharply in 1933. In the case of road works and social and public services, expenditure rose in the first two years of depression but then both became destabilising, especially the former, which fell from a peak of £22.9 million in 1931 to £9.8 million in 1933 (1930 prices). The only form of investment to remain unscathed was that in electricity supply which rose steadily throughout the depression. From the mid-1930s most forms of public investment were rising and continued to do so until the end of the decade.

Local authorities accounted for a fairly large proportion of public investment, more particularly in dwellings, roads, and social and public services. In all the main downswings, 1921, 1929–32 and 1938, capital spending of local authorities tended to rise and therefore exerted a stabilising influence. But there were offsetting factors to be taken into account. In general, the expansionary influence of municipal spending was fairly slight, partly because expenditure out of borrowed money was largely offset by simultaneous repayments and accumulations out of revenue. Second, local authorities did not maintain their spending in the early phase of recovery. Third, there was very little attempt to concentrate expenditure in those areas with the worst unemployment.

It is apparent that there was never any serious attempt to develop an active counter-cyclical policy, or to carry through a large-scale programme of public works, least of all in the early 1930s. However, although adherence to the doctrine of the balanced budget effectively constrained the use to which fiscal policy could be put, this did not necessarily mean that it was always a destabilising force. Various categories of expenditure — transfer payments, public investment and government spending as a whole — tended to rise or increase in relative importance in the depression years of 1921, 1929–32 and 1938. These upward shifts exerted a moderating influence on the downswings. Unfortunately, they were far too small to have much effect and were offset to a large extent by compensatory tax increases as in 1931–32.

Study Questions on Public Finance

(a) What were the main sources of government revenue in the interwar period?
(b) Write a critical account of the government's fiscal policy in the interwar years.
(c) Discuss the importance of public investment.

Recommended Reading on Public Finance

Hicks, U.K., *The Finance of British Government, 1920–1936* (London, 1938)
Peacock, A.T. and Wiseman, J., *The Growth of Public Expenditure in the United Kingdom*, (London, 1961)
Sabine, B.E.V., *British Budgets in Peace and War, 1932–1945* (London, 1970)

15 Prices, Wages, Incomes and Employment

The biggest problem in the interwar period was, of course, unemployment which was only partly offset by increased welfare payments. Thus at best an index of real wages can measure only changes in the wage earnings of those in continuous employment when expressed in a 'composite unit of consumables'. Clearly there is no single indicator which measures accurately changes in living standards of the population as a whole. Certainly movements in wage indices will give a broad idea of the dimensions of improvement or deterioration, always bearing in mind the many variations from the average, and also the fact that these figures apply only to people actually in employment.

The key data on wages and earnings are listed in Table 17. The first column is an index of average annual earnings of all wage and salary earners, while the second refers to wage earners only and covers mining, manufacturing, building, transport and some services. The third column contains an index of average wage rates paid to employees mainly in industrial occupations. All three show a broad degree of similarity in their movements. There was a strong and sustained rise during the war and immediately

Table 17 Indices of Money Wages, Real Wages, Employment and Retail Prices, 1913, 1919–38 (1930 = 100)

	Average Annual Earnings	Average Annual Wage Earnings	Weekly Wage Rates	Retail Prices (cost of living index)	Average Annual Real Wage Earnings	Total Employment	Unemployment Percentage (insured workers)
	(1)	(2)	(3)	(4)	(5)	(6)	(7)
1913	–	52.4	53.2	63.3	82.8	–	2.1
1919	–	–	122.3	136.1	–	–	2.1
1920	132.5	143.7	146.8	157.1	91.2	107.1	2.0
1921	126.6	134.6	145.7	143.0	94.1	91.7	17.1
1922	106.0	107.9	111.7	115.8	93.2	92.4	13.6
1923	99.5	100.0	100.0	110.1	90.8	94.4	11.2
1924	100.5	101.5	102.1	110.8	91.6	95.7	10.0
1925	101.1	102.2	102.1	111.4	91.7	96.8	11.1
1926	100.1	99.3	102.1	108.9	91.2	94.2	12.3
1927	100.8	101.5	102.1	106.0	95.8	100.1	9.4
1928	100.0	100.1	102.1	105.1	95.2	100.6	10.5
1929	100.2	100.4	101.1	103.8	96.7	102.3	10.0
1930	100.0	100.0	100.0	100.0	100.0	100.0	16.4
1931	98.6	98.2	98.9	93.4	105.1	97.2	21.2
1932	97.0	96.3	97.9	91.1	105.7	97.6	21.8
1933	96.4	95.3	95.7	88.6	107.6	100.1	19.2
1934	97.4	96.4	95.7	89.2	108.1	103.5	16.3
1935	98.8	98.0	96.8	90.5	108.3	105.7	15.0
1936	100.7	100.2	98.9	93.0	107.7	109.5	12.5
1937	102.6	102.8	103.2	97.5	105.4	113.8	10.3
1938	105.7	106.3	106.4	98.7	107.7	114.0	12.3

Sources: Col.1 A.L. Chapman and R. Knight, *Wages and Salaries in the United Kingdom 1920–1938* (Cambridge, 1953), p. 30

Col.2 E.H. Phelps Brown and Margaret Browne, *A Century of Pay* (London, 1968), p. 399 and Appendix 3, UK, Col.1

Col.3 *London and Cambridge Economic Bulletin*, 44 (December 1962), p. xiii

Col.4 B.R. Mitchell and Phyllis Deane, *Abstract of British Historical Statistics* (Cambridge, 1962), p. 478

Col.5 Col.2 converted into real terms using cost of living index (col.4) as deflator
Col.6 Chapman and Knight, *op. cit.*, pp. 32–3
Col.7 1921–38, E.M. Burns, *British Unemployment Programs, 1920–1938* (Washington, 1941), p. 343. Before 1921, London and Cambridge Economic Service, *The British Economy: Key Statistics, 1900–1966* (1967), Table E, p. 8

thereafter; by 1918 wages and earnings were roughly double the prewar level and in the postwar boom they rose to two-and-one-half to three times above the 1913 base. The somewhat lower peak in total earnings (column 1) in 1920 can largely be accounted for by the lag in salary earnings behind wages. Then came a dramatic collapse which lasted until well into 1923, by which time wages and earnings had fallen to slightly under twice their 1913 levels. After these violent fluctuations movements in wages were very modest indeed. They remained remarkably stable until 1930 when a downward trend set in. But the decline was very moderate compared with that of postwar and was checked in 1934. Thereafter wages rose slowly until 1938 when they were about 5 or 6 per cent higher than in 1930 and just about double the prewar level.

During the 1920s and 1930s earnings and wages moved cyclically, though with some lag behind the turning points in business activity. However, cyclical conformity was greater after 1929 than in the 1920s apart from the immediate postwar years. Between 1923 and 1929 wages remained very stable, despite the fact that employment and output expanded more or less continuously.

Wages fluctuated with unemployment in the interwar period, but probably of equal importance in determining wages was the downward trend in prices which was almost continuous from 1920 to 1933–34. This created a hard market environment for the acceptance of wage claims and during the times of very high unemployment, as in the early 1920s and early 1930s, the imposition of wage cuts was relatively easy. At the peak of the postwar boom the level of costs and prices was regarded as abnormal, while unit wage costs were high in relation to market prices. Once the price boom broke however it was possible to force down wages under sliding scale agreements,[1] though not without considerable industrial strife. Thus of the aggregate reductions in rates, 55 per cent in 1921 and 38 per cent in 1922, were made under sliding scale agreements of this sort. After 1921–22, sagging prices at a time of relatively high unit costs in British industry provided for a period of relative wage stability.

The fall in money wages in the early 1930s was only to be expected given the high level of unemployment, the decline in business activity and the accelerated downward trend in prices. In comparison, however, wages and earnings declined very much less than in the United States and Germany, and compared with the postwar collapse the decline of 5 per cent between 1929 and 1933 looks very moderate indeed. In part this can be accounted for by the relative mildness of the British slump and the greater strength of the trade unions.

Despite a high level of unemployment throughout the 1930s, wages advanced fairly steadily in the later 1930s. In the main cyclical forces were the chief determinant of wage movements, though the latter did not react quickly to changes in business activity. Changes in unemployment and prices, especially the latter in the long term, were the main factors at work. There were, in addition, long-term forces making for an increase in the average level of incomes from employment. The redistribution of income in favour of labour raised the average level of earnings of employed workers. Most of the gain accrued to salary workers. There was a marked increase in the number of salaried workers; between 1911 and 1938 the number increased from 1.67 million to 3.84 million and the

---

1. A wage system in which the rate paid varies with changes in the cost of living, or with the price of a particular commodity; it was especially common in the coal industry where wages were linked to the price of coal.

ratio of wage to salaried workers fell from 9:1 to 4:1. The total wage bill remained fairly constant in terms of national income at a time when the proportion of wage earners to total employment was declining.

Over the period 1913 to 1938 average annual wages rose by 103 per cent, an increase which was very similar to that in income per capita of the whole population. Salary earnings rose somewhat less, probably by between 70 and 75 per cent. Most of the rise in employment incomes occurred during the war and postwar boom. Between 1924 and the end of the 1930s wages rose by only about 5 per cent while salary earnings fell slightly. Income per capita however rose by 12.6 per cent in these years. In the period 1939–45 average weekly wage rates rose considerably. Wage rates were approximately 6 per cent higher in 1939 than in 1924 and by the end of the war they had reached about 61 per cent more than the 1924 level.

Real earnings of wage earners rose quite significantly between 1913 and 1920–21, after which they fell slightly and then remained stable until the late 1920s. The upward movement was somewhat erratic, with most of the gain occurring in the periods 1926–27 and 1929–31. By 1938 average real wage earnings were some 30 per cent higher than in 1913. This gain was unevenly distributed over time however; a considerable increase in real wages took place between 1913 and the early 1920s, and from then to 1938 they increased by less than 15 per cent.

For the period 1939–41 real earnings showed a substantial increase even though wage rates rose more slowly than the cost of living. The increase of 81 per cent in money earnings was largely due to longer hours and the harder or more skilled work required by the war economy. Prices began to increase even in 1939 as a result of rising commodity prices and a rise in freights. These were promptly followed by pressure for wage increases. To counteract these wage claims, in 1940 subsidisation of a wide rage of foodstuffs began to be accepted. This subsidy policy was extended and strengthened throughout the war years. However the cost of living continued to increase; by 1941 it was 26 per cent above the 1939 level, but by 1945 it had advanced only 5 percentage points further. Wage rates also continued to rise; they were 20 per cent higher in 1941 than in 1939 and almost 50 per cent above the 1939 level in 1945, having overtaken the cost of living in 1942.

After allowing for price fluctuations and the increase in population of the interwar years, it is possible to arrive at a measure of real income per head for the whole population. There was practically no increase in real income per head for the period 1914–24. In the mid-1920s real income per head showed a fair degree of stability around £45 per annum (at 1900 prices). This increased appreciably to approximately £50 per annum in the boom years of 1928–29. Although money incomes declined during the depression years, the British people were able to maintain their 'real' standard of living due to the collapse in the values of international primary products. By 1934 real income per head had increased to £54 per annum, well above the 1929 levels. It rose still further to 1938, at which time the average Briton was approximately 30 per cent better off than in 1913. During the Second World War real income per head probably rose slightly, though most of the gain accrued to the wage earning classes whose earnings rose faster than the cost of living. However, rationing and scarcities arising from wartime conditions led to a drastic reduction in civilian consumption with the result that savings ratios rose considerably. After adjusting the value of goods and services bought in 1944 at their 1938 prices, real consumption in the later year was approximately 80 per cent of the 1938 level.

Study Questions on Prices, Wages, Incomes and Employment

(a) Why did prices decline or stagnate for much of the period?
(b) Why did real wages increase during the interwar years?
(c) Why did money wages fall sharply between 1920 and 1923?

Recommended Reading on Prices, Wages, Incomes and Employment

Bowley, A.L., *Wages and Income in the United Kingdom since 1860* (London, 1937)

Burnett, J., *A History of the Cost of Living* (Middlesex, 1969)

Phelps Brown, E.H. and Browne, M., *A Century of Pay* (London, 1968)

Routh, G., *Occupation and Pay in Great Britain, 1906–60* (Cambridge, 1965)

16 Social Policy and Material Welfare

Though the basic outlines of the modern welfare state were developed early in the twentieth century, up to the First World War the level of social expenditure per head remained very small. After the war there were considerable pressures to extend the new state services, not the least of which was the persistent unemployment. The approach then was to expand existing services and even to introduce new ones. Thus unemployment insurance, which covered a rather limited number of occupations before the war, was greatly extended in 1920 to include 11 million people. Further trades were brought in during the course of the interwar years, so that by 1938 it embraced 15.4 million people. Similarly, the scope of the health service was extended, though originally its coverage had been wider than the other schemes; by 1939 it included some 20 million people compared with 15 million in 1921. Yet this still left nearly as many dependents outside the scheme unprotected against distress and sickness. The third prewar scheme, that of old age pensions, was not changed in principle, but payments were raised to 10s per week and the income limits were increased. In addition, a new contributory pension scheme, together with allowances for widows and orphans, was inaugurated in 1925. By 1937 some 20 million people were covered under the legislation of 1925 and over three million were already receiving benefits.

Other public services, the most important being education, child care and housing, were extended or improved in the period. Though facilities in schools were improved — for example, by the widening of curricula and the reduction in the number of oversized classes — there still remained much scope for further progress. Fisher's Education Act of 1918 was a step in the right direction, but even this legislation fell foul of economy cuts. It proved impossible to push the school leaving age beyond 14, while higher education remained very much the preserve of the rich. Perhaps the most promising area of success was in housing where intervention occurred on a large scale. Local authorities built over one million houses which were mostly for letting to low income families, while in the 1920s private builders received Treasury subsidies.

Total government expenditure on all social services in monetary terms rose from £101 million in 1913 to £438 million in 1929 and to £596 million in 1938, equivalent respectively to 4.1, 9.5 and 11.3 per cent of the gross national product. In per capita terms the expenditure amounted to £12.5 in 1938, compared with £9.6 in 1929 and £2.2 in 1913. After allowing for price changes this represented a more than three-fold increase between 1913 and 1938. By the end of the interwar period the redistribution of income was at a higher level than in any previous year, though the total effect was relatively small. If, for instance, the level of unemployment in 1937 (1.5 million) had been reduced by about one-half this would have raised the national income by the same amount as the amount redistributed. Also, the redistributive effect was modified in several ways. For one thing, both rich and poor stood to gain from social services. In fact in some cases, notably education and housing, it was the better-off manual workers and the middle classes who gained most. Secondly, some of the welfare schemes were financed in part by the workers themselves.

The movement towards a more even income distribution was very moderate in the interwar period. The levelling up process appears to have been confined largely to the middle and lower income bands, since the top income bracket maintained its share fairly well. In 1938, 55.5 per cent of distributed personal income before tax was shared among 87.2 per cent of the income recipients all earning less than £250 a year (that is the working classes), while the remaining 44.5 per cent went to 12.8 per cent of the income receivers with earnings over £250 a year. Furthermore, the top one per cent of the income receivers (over £500 a year) absorbed 29 per cent of the total distributed. A partial analysis by Stamp[1] for 1914 gives a breakdown of 45 per cent to 5½ per cent of the people with separate incomes, leaving 55 per cent to be shared among 95 per cent of income recipients, while the top one per cent accounted for about 30 per cent of total income.

The lower income groups were the main beneficiaries of social transfer payments, and the net effect was that the incomes of the working classes (under £250 a year) were raised by between 8 and 10 per cent through redistribution, the bulk of the gain going to those with incomes of less than £125 per annum. In turn, the incomes of the middle and upper classes were reduced by between 10 and 18 per cent. Changes in direct taxation also had some impact in the right direction. In 1938 the lower income groups (less than £250 a year) absorbed 59.6 per cent of the post-tax distributed personal incomes, as against 55.5 per cent before tax, while those on incomes above this limit now retained only just over 40 per cent. The share of the top one per cent of the income recipients was reduced from 29 to about 24.4 per cent. The share absorbed by the intermediate range incomes, that is, between £250 and £500, remained practically stable at 16 per cent both before and after tax.

Despite the vast extensions of social services, benefits, especially for the unemployed, often fell short of human needs, while many of those who had exhausted their in-

---

1. Sir Josiah Stamp, *Wealth and Taxable Capacity* (1922), p. 87.

surance claims were forced on to means test assistance and poor relief. As late as 1936 some 330,000 persons were on poor relief and another 600,000 on means test assistance. This brings us to the problem of poverty.

During the interwar period there was a significant increase in real incomes and real wages and on the whole the nation was better fed, clothed and housed than before the war. The national health and physical well-being of the population improved — death rates declined, the expectation of life was much higher than at the end of the nineteenth century, while children were on average taller and healthier than their parents had been.

However, poverty persisted. A substantial proportion of the population was living in some state of poverty. At a guess the proportion might be between 20 and 30 per cent, while possibly up to one-half was deficient in vitamins. Families living below the poverty line might have been able to afford an adequate diet, but only at the expense of other necessities such as clothing and shelter. In other cases, ignorance, prejudice, lack of time and lack of facilities might have prevented a nutritionally adequate diet. Moreover, many families with incomes which allowed a level of subsistence above the poverty line had little to spare for luxuries and next to nothing to fall back on in times of need or unexpected crisis.

The problem of poverty and distress was greater in the northern half of the country including Scotland and in Wales than it was in the South. Here unemployment was higher and more prolonged, incomes were lower and living conditions, especially housing, less congenial than in London and the South. Unemployment was by no means the only cause of poverty. About one-third could be attributed to unemployment and inadequate benefits, perhaps another third to inadequate earnings even though employment was regular, while a further 16 per cent was caused by the problem of old age.

In contrast to the poverty experienced by some, were the higher real earnings, more leisure, improved living conditions and better social amenities enjoyed by a substantial proportion of the population. Hours of work were

An interwar London slum. Poverty persisted as a problem for 20 to 30 per cent of the population, despite the improved living conditions of the majority.

SOCIAL POLICY AND MATERIAL WELFARE

reduced substantially shortly after the First World War as a result of the eight hour day movement. In 1919, 6½ million workers obtained reductions averaging 6½ hours a week without loss of pay, while in the following year a further half million or so were similarly affected. This reduced the average working week to around 48 hours or less compared with 53–54 before the war. For most workers in the interwar period there was in total an 11 per cent reduction in nominal working hours. The total gain to workers can be estimated by converting that part taken out in the form of shorter hours into real terms and adding it to the increase in real earnings; between 1913 and 1938 this amounted to a total increase of 46.3 per cent on the base year, 30 percentage points being in the form of increased real earnings and the remainder representing a bonus in the form of leisure.

In addition to the reduction in working hours, there were also increases in holidays. It has been estimated that in 1937 the number of holidaymakers away for a week or more was about 15 million and most of this increase had taken place since 1919. It owed little, however, to the holidays with pay movement, since in 1937 only about four million workers out of a total working population of 18½ million had paid annual leave. Partly as a result of the Holidays with Pay Act of 1938 there was a sudden jump in the numbers receiving paid holidays. By the middle of 1939 some 11 million workers were covered by various agreements.

One aspect of social changes not yet considered is the trade union movement. Trade union membership grew rapidly during the First World War and reached a peak of 8 million by 1920, twice the number it had been in 1914. In the interwar period trade union strength fluctuated with the changing economic conditions. In the depressed years of the 1920s and early 1930s membership declined, but it began to pick up in the mid-1930s and by 1939 it reached 6¼ million, still well below the 1920 peak figure. By 1943 the 1920 figure was passed and membership in 1946 totalled 8.8 million.

The First World War required co-operation between the

government and the trade unions; in 1914 the latter agreed to a policy of compulsory arbitration. In each of the three years 1915, 1916 and 1917 there was only one major industrial dispute. After the war, however, major disputes reappeared. In 1926, the Trades Union Congress called a General Strike in support of the coalminers. All except key workers were called out and after ten days the TUC ordered a return to work. The strike had failed, since the government could supply essential services and because union leaders were not unanimous in their aims.

For the remainder of the interwar period the opportunities for strike action were substantially reduced due to economic depression and unemployment. Full employment returned in the Second World War and again co-operation between government and trade unions meant that there were no major industrial disputes. There was close co-operation between the trade unions and the Minister for Labour, Ernest Bevin, in schemes to increase production. After the war the trade union movement emerged as an important part of industrial decisions.

Study Questions on Social Policy and Material Welfare

(a) Can the advances in social welfare policy be regarded as significant?

(b) What contribution did welfare policy make to the standard of living?

(c) What were the main causes of poverty in the period?

Recommended Reading on Social Policy and Material Welfare

Barna, T., *The Redistribution of Incomes through Public Finance in 1937* (Oxford, 1945)
Gilbert, B.B., *British Social Policy 1914–1939* (London, 1970)
Titmuss, R.M., *Poverty and Population* (London, 1938)

17 Life and Leisure in a Two Nation World

In the social, no less than the economic, sphere, there were quite fundamental changes taking place during the interwar period. While war, depression and above all persistent unemployment bred a feeling of insecurity, for the vast majority of the population it was a time of improved living standards, a more varied diet, better health and improved environmental conditions. In a broader context the interwar period also offered a wide range of new opportunities in domestic living habits, in the pursuit of leisure activities, together with a relaxation of the rigid and moral codes of social behaviour of the Victorian and Edwardian eras. In fact, one could say that this period marked the beginning of the social revolution towards the permissive society of today.

Rising real incomes, a shift in consumption patterns, a decline in the size of families and an increasing number of working wives, meant that the average family had more money to spend on home comforts and leisure activities. The average family size fell from 4.35 to 3.59 persons between 1911 and 1939, and by the end of the 1930s the average working class family spent 35 and 9 per cent respectively of its income on food, and rent and rates, as against 60 and 16 per cent in 1914. There was, moreover, a sharp fall in the per capita consumption of alcohol during the period. Thus despite a general improvement in dietary patterns — the consumption of fruit and vegetables and eggs and dairy products rose considerably during the period — there was more money to spend on housing and furnishings. With the buildings of over four million new houses during the interwar years many people, including the better-off working class, were buying their own homes, moving into new council accommodation, or 'filtering-up' into better quality second-hand accommodation. This generated a demand for new furnishings, electrical goods and consumer durables, the latter being stimulated by the widespread use of electricity. The number of electricity consumers rose from 730,000 in 1920 to around nine million in the late 1930s, when two out of every three houses were wired for electric power, as against one in seventeen at the beginning of the period. Thus by the end of the period the majority of households owned an electric iron and radio, one in seven a vacuum cleaner and electric cooker and one in fifty a refrigerator and washing machine.

It was of course only the beginning of the domestic revolution in the home, though a foretaste of what was to come when the supply of domestic servants dried up. The more sophisticated consumer durables were confined largely to the wealthier middle class homes, while fitted carpets, central heating and the use of a telephone were still something of a rarity. Many housewives had to be content with fitted linoleum, a new cooking range, an electric iron, possibly a wash boiler and new furnishings and fittings, more often than not bought on hire purchase. Nevertheless, as Pollard has pointed out,[1] the bare statistics often fail to take account fully of the difference made by electric light instead of candles, or gas and electric cookers instead of coal and coke ranges, of improved housing amenities generally including indoor water and sanitation,

---

1. S. Pollard, *The Development of the British Economy, 1914–1950* (London, 1962), p. 293.

and the radio, cinema and newspapers within nearly everyone's reach. Moreover, for many who moved into new houses it meant an escape from the grimy and congested living conditions in or near the city centres to pleasant suburban surroundings on the new housing estates with gardens and recreational facilities.

Shopping habits were also changing steadily, though the big revolution in service trades was to await a later date. The corner or suburban shop still dominated the scene, but the growth of multiple- and chain-store retailing, including such famous names as Woolworth, Marks and Spencer, Sainsbury, Lipton, Burton and Boots, offered the customer a much wider range of branded and non-branded goods, including food, clothing, cosmetics and all types of household products. They advertised and promoted their goods extensively, they were cheaper than the smaller stores, and often they granted credit facilities. (See also on the subject of multiple- and chain-store retailing Chapter 9.)

But perhaps the most dramatic developments were in the field of leisure and recreational pursuits. Compared with Victorian and Edwardian England, the working man, no less than his wealthier middle class counterpart, was literally bombarded with opportunities for filling in his increased spare time following the reductions in hours of work. The diehard puritanicals might frown upon the apparent decay in moral values as the growing popular press titillated the baser instincts of its readers with stories of brutal murders or sex scandals, or reported the goings-on of the bright young things who spent the night at riotous parties or jazz concerts, but at least they might take consolation from the fact that the sobriety of the population was improving; people were drinking less partly as a result of a reduction in the strength of beer and the rise in the costs of spirits, while the public house had to compete with alternative outlets for the population's leisure time. The traditional public house remained the domain of the working man, but new lounges and cocktail bars were springing up in the suburbs and counties to cater for the wealthier, car-owning fraternity who demanded something better than the 'spit and sawdust' saloon.

If the drink problem was abating in this period social reformers had a new issue to worry about, namely the craze for gambling. Betting on horses had of course been common before 1914 and it was not confined to any one social group. After the war horse-racing was joined by greyhound-racing and football pools as alternative betting outlets and the stage was set for a punter's paradise. Gambling became big business for the promoters and it is safe to assume that the majority of the population were betting fairly regularly. By the later 1930s some 10 million people were returning football coupons comprising a total stake each week of £40 million. Many of the stakes were of course fairly small and the alarmist reports that the working classes were frittering away their wages in an unseemly way are no doubt exaggerated. For most people it was simply the case of a small 'flutter' which helped to relieve the monotony of work, with the prospoect of glittering prizes providing a temporary escape into a dream world. In 1931 one pools winner netted no less than £345,000.

That the interwar years were rich in entertainment and sport is evidenced by the fact that employment in these trades rose from 101.7 to 247.9 thousand between 1920 and 1938. For the more sober-minded citizen there were more innocuous ways than gambling for spending one's money and leisure time. There was a profusion of reading material available, including popular newspapers, magazines and a flood of new novels. Less mentally taxing was listening to the radio which became the pastime of the millions — by the end of the period there were nine million receivers in operation — the novelty of which compensated for the rather straitlaced programmes fed out by the BBC under the puritanical direction of Lord Reith, though by the early 1930s the beginnings of commercial radio promised to offer an alternative and somewhat lighter diet to which the BBC responded in due course. The radiogram also offered another source of fireside entertainment. Outside the home the cinema was a strong rival attraction, particularly for the younger members of society. Though

London's latest cinema, 'The Granada', Tooting, in 1937, extravagantly designed to look like a secular cathedral. Cinema was the most popular form of mass entertainment in the inter-war years.

variety theatres and music-halls were still popular, they could not compete with the cinema in drawing the crowds. By 1939, when the number of cinemas was approaching 5000, weekly attendances were running at 20 million. It was by far the most popular form of mass entertainment. Nor is it surprising that it became so popular given the dramatic improvement in the quality of production, from silent films shown in garrick-like buildings to the 'talkies' and colour films exhibited in the big luxurious cinemas of the 1930s with their exotic-sounding names — the Rialto, Ritz, Roxy — and plush interiors, and the added attraction of refreshment and musical entertainment at the intervals. Countless millions no doubt flocked to the cinema for a few hours to escape the harsh realities of life and to see their favourite 'stars'.

Despite the attractions of the 'silver screen', dancing became a serious rival to the cinema in this period. The relaxation of moral codes of behaviour, the revolution in women's attire, and the 'explosion of high spirits' following the war led to a boom in mixed gatherings at dance-halls, the impetus strengthened no doubt by the popularity of the famous big bands of this era. Nearly every town of any worthwhile size sported its own dance hall with entertainment for both old and young alike, and the dancing craze was given added zest by the introduction of several new and unconventional dances — the 'Jog Trot', the 'Vampire', the 'Shimmy', the 'Charleston' and the 'Black Bottom' — which shocked the puritanical but gave endless pleasure to the younger clientele.

Sport too was booming in this period, but more as a passive spectator event rather than in terms of the number of active participants, though the latter were certainly increasing. Nearly all forms of sports increased in popularity and two new evening sports, greyhound-racing and speedway-racing, swelled the ranks of the traditional sports of football, cricket, boxing, tennis, swimming, golf, bowls and archery. Many of them became national spectator sports with substantial increases in attendances, though there were clear class distinctions involved. Football, for example, remained very much a proletarian reserve, both for spectators and players, the latter being paid in line with the skilled working man rather than the superstars of today. Greyhound-racing and boxing likewise were essentially working class activities, the latter having a rather unenviable reputation for brutality until regulated from 1934 onwards. By contrast, tennis, golf, cricket and motor racing were essentially middle class sports, particularly in terms of active participation since the costs of playing were beyond the average working class pocket, and in any case each had its own exclusive appeal for those concerned with social cachets.

Some of the above activities undoubtedly benefited from the motoring revolution which did much to increase personal mobility. The horse-drawn era was drawing to a close during these years as countless cars, lorries, coaches (charabancs) and motor cycles invaded the streets and roads of the country. By 1939 there were some 1.9 million private cars in use, over one million lorries, vans and coaches and nearly half a million motor cycles. Despite the sharp fall in the price of cars, private motoring remained the preserve of the wealthier sections of society. The working man usually had to make do with a motor cycle, a bicycle, or failing either he could use public transport, the omnibus for routine short journeys and the charabanc for pleasure outings. The enormous growth in bus and coach travel, which came to rival the railways by the end of the period, points to a much greater degree of mobility among the working population. Motor transport in general, whether private or public, gave much greater scope for pleasure trips to remote rural areas and seaside resorts, and as J.B. Priestley noted in his *English Journey*, few places were safe from the coach-tripper. Seaside resorts too were inundated by enthusiastic holidaymakers as the practice of taking annual holidays became widespread. Since 1919 the number of holidaymakers had increased dramatically, so that by 1937, 15 million people spent a week or more away from home, a trend which was further boosted by the Holidays with Pay Act of 1938. (See also on this subject the previous chapter.) The increasing popularity of holidaymaking, whether annual, weekend or daytrips, led to a rapid growth of business in seaside resorts. By the end of the 1930s no less than 20 million visitors were recorded at Britain's seaside resorts, Blackpool leading the way with seven million, followed by Southend with 5½ million and Hastings with three million. Many of the visitors were no doubt 'day-trippers', though each resort catered for a regular clientele during the high season. Compared with the free and easy atmosphere of today's packaged holiday abroad, the disciplinary rigours of seaside lodgings administered by the immortal landlady must have been something of an ordeal, but at least it provided countless millions with the first opportunity to take a much needed break from the routine of everyday life.

In a quiet and more sedate fashion there were several other outdoor activities which flourished and attracted a select band of adherents or enthusiasts, more often the younger members of society. Cycling as a pastime and recreational pursuit continued to be popular, with many clubs springing up to cater for the needs of the regular cyclist, while hiking, rambling, walking and other 'keep-fit' activities became increasingly popular ways of spending leisure time, with beneficial effects in terms of health. Though still confined to a minority of the population, these pursuits attracted a not inconsiderable number of supporters. By 1939, for example, the Youth Hostels Association, founded in 1930, had over 100,000 registered members and 400 hostels with some one million overnight bookings being recorded in that year.

With so many exciting changes taking place on the social scene it is difficult sometimes to believe that there was another face to society. Yet if for many it could be described as a 'golden age' in terms of living standards and opportunities to partake of pleasure and entertainment, one should never forget that a sizeable fraction of the population was not in any position to enjoy the fruits of the consumer society. While social investigators could report that the degree of poverty had diminished since the Edwardian period, and while calculations suggest that the unemployed married man on the dole in the 1930s was better off than many a fully employed labourer in 1900, the fact remains that there existed a submerged segment of the population who lived in poverty and distress for one reason or another, be it low earnings, unemployment, too many children or sickness and old age. The presence of poverty was real enough and, as might be expected, its incidence was greater in the northern regions because of their serious unemployment problem. For these unfortunate people it was not a question of trips to the seaside, cinema visits, sports participation ,or the puchase of modern appliances and home comforts; rather it was how to keep body and soul together on the most meagre of incomes. They were the characters immortalised in the famous novels and writings of the period, especially Walter Greenwood's *Love on the Dole* and George Orwell's *The Road to Wigan Pier*. It was a world apart from the mass of the population, and even more so from the world inhabited by the characters portrayed in the writings of Evelyn Waugh and P.G. Wodehouse. Britain was still a two nation country.

Yet Orwell and Greenwood's descriptions were accurate if not necessarily representative of the mass of society. While the social investigations of the period recorded general improvement, they also confirmed that grinding poverty still existed. First hand accounts illustrate vividly what the struggle for existence meant in practical terms. A miner from Crook who had been unemployed since 1927 described his family's experience as follows:

'It's just over seven years since I was stood off and we've lived on about thirty-six bob during that time, that's me and the wife and the six kids. The rent's not bad, eight and six, but it's replacing breakages, clothing, extra nourishment for the kids and furniture that we find difficult to get. I've a bit of an allotment that brings us potatoes and cabbages but we don't often get meat and as for fruit you just can't buy it.'[2]

---

2. J. Newsom, *Out of the Pit* (London, 1936), p. 20. For a similar contemporary recollection, see M. Cohen, *I Was One of the Unemployed* (London, 1945).

Wal Hannington's case studies demonstrate not only the absence of modern comforts in the homes of the very poor, but also the virtual absence of the bare necessities. Take the case of Mrs. E.M.W. of Pontypool, Monmouth:

> 'There are nine in the family, the ages in the family being fourteen, thirteen, eleven, seven, five, three, and two. The income from all sources is £2 7s. a week. Living-conditions in the home are that all food has to be cooked on the open fire — there is no gas stove or oven. There is only one small cupboard for food and no meat safe. In regard to cooking utensils, the family has only one kettle, one small frying-pan, two small saucepans. Utensils for preparing food consist of only one bowl, which is used for making puddings and to wash up in. They have only seven cups and saucers between nine persons, two knives, six small spoons, six forks, and eight plates. The family live in three rooms, one living-kitchen and two small bedrooms. The kitchen has a stone floor and the bedrooms have bare boards; no lino. There are two full-size beds and one small bed. In bedclothes the family have only two flannelette blankets on each bed, one quilt and one sheet, three pillow-cases. All bed-clothing is very threadbare and has little warmth. The small bed does not belong to them; they have it only on loan. Four boys sleep in one bed and two boys sleep in the small bed. Husband and wife and child two years of age sleep in the other bed. The springs in one of the beds are badly broken and there is no money to get a new mattress. The house is old and very damp and cold.'[3]

These cases are by no means isolated examples as the contemporary accounts will testify. Such desperate conditions often led to moral degradation and in some cases the break-up of the family.

Despite the plight of a significant minority of the population, British society was never threatened by social explosion during this period. True there were many demonstrations about social conditions, the most famous of which were the hunger marches, but the social order remained intact while political extremism was conspicuous by its absence. At first sight this may appear surpris-

---

3. W. Hannington, *The Problem of the Distressed Areas* (London, 1937), p. 67.

ing when one reads the horrific accounts of life at its worst in this period. But on deeper reflection the absence of anything approaching social revolution is not difficult to explain. For one thing the majority of the population experienced considerable improvement in material well-being during this period and their social conscience was weak and therefore had little real influence. The poverty-stricken were in a minority, they were isolated in time and space, and they had little power to organise effective protest, let alone create a social revolution. Moreover, at various points in time the situation was diffused by public relief in the form of unemployment benefit, poor relief, free school meals, free milk, improved hospital services and the like. Such measures would seem to have been effective in allaying any incipient discontent, at least insofar as one may judge from contemporary accounts. Our miner from Crook admitted that: 'At first I used to feel bitter and want to do something violent. I suppose if conditions worsened we might risk it .... but as long as you've got the dole regular, well, you think twice before doing something militant.'[4] Similarly, an unemployed engineer in the 1930s told a reporter that 'Unemployment benefit is not enough so's you can live like you're used to living ... But we get enough to keep us healthy, and you can't ask for much more, now, can you?'[5] The reporter went on to explain that 'The plain fact appears to be that there has been brought into the worker's life, even when he is unemployed, a sufficient degree of security, so that talk of undermining the social order which gives him that small degree of security is an interesting debating opportunity rather than a vital discussion of actual possibilities.'[6] George Orwell had a different explanation. While deploring the cult of cheap luxuries at the expense of necessities of life such as food, he admitted that they did have a

---

4. Newsom *op. cit.*, p.20.
5. E.W. Bakke, *The Unemployed Man* (London, 1933), quoted in S. Constantine, *Unemployment in Britain between the Wars*, (London, 1980), p.31.
6. *Ibid.*, p. 43.

therapeutic effect: 'It is quite likely that fish-and-chips, artsilk stockings, tinned salmon, cut-price chocolates ... the movies, the radio, strong tea and the football pools have between them averted revolution.'[7]

Study Questions on Life and Leisure in a Two Nation World

(a) Discuss some of the main changes in domestic living conditions during the interwar years.

(b) Explain the growth in the provision of leisure activities.

(c) How was political and social protest contained?

Recommended Reading on Life and Leisure in a Two Nation World

Graves, R. and Hodge, A., *The Long Weekend: A Social History of Great Britain, 1918–1939* (London, 1940)

Marwick, A., *Britain in the Century of Total War: War, Peace and Social Change, 1900–1967* (London, 1968)

Stevenson, J., *Social Conditions in Britain between the Wars* (Harmondsworth, 1977)

---

7. G. Orwell, *The Road to Wigan Pier* (Harmondsworth, 1972 edn), pp. 80–81, quoted in J. Stevenson, *Social Conditions in Britain Between the Wars* (Harmondsworth, 1977), p. 24.

18 Unemployment and Economic Policy

The interwar years are best remembered for their high and sustained level of unemployment. In fact unemployment was rife everywhere during this period, but Britain suffered more severely than most other countries. Throughout the period unemployment very rarely fell below 10 per cent of the insured labour force and at its peak, in the third quarter of 1932, it rose to nearly 23 per cent. It is true that the data from the insurance returns exaggerate the relative importance of the problem, since the incidence of unemployment among non-insured workers was lower than for the insured. If allowance is made for this factor, then the real unemployment rates for the 1920s and 1930s work out at 7.5 and 11.5 per cent respectively compared with 12.1 and 16.5 per cent for insured workers only. Even after these adjustments however, unemployment on average was probably about twice as large as it had been before 1914, while the absolute numbers leave one in no doubt as to the magnitude of the problem. In the best years some one million people were without work, at the depth of the depression nearly three million, while many more were on short-time. It was not until the early 1980s that unemployment on this scale re-occurred.

One of the chief characteristics of unemployment was the great disparity in its incidence both between regions and within regions. In broad terms the North of the country suffered very much more than the South. Unemployment in the South including the Midlands, was about half that of outer Britain (the North-east, Northwest, Scotland, Wales and Northern Ireland), with extremes ranging from 23.54 per cent in Wales and 19 per cent in Scotland between 1923 and 1938, to 8.48 per cent in London and almost 9 per cent in the South-east. This in fact was a complete reversal of the situation before the war, when the southern half of the country recorded higher unemployment rates than the north. The trade union figures, though very incomplete, suggest a rate of 8.7 per cent for London and 4.7 per cent in the South-east in 1912–13, as against 2.6 per cent in the North of England, 3.1 per cent in Wales and only 1.8 per cent in Scotland. (This was largely due to itinerant unemployed labour in the South, and the strength of the old staple industries in the North, Wales and Scotland.)

The regional disparity between North and South tended to widen during the course of the interwar years. There were however marked variations within regions of both high and low unemployment. The relatively prosperous South had some counties which suffered badly, notably Norfolk, Suffolk, Cornwall, Devon and Gloucester, while in the North, Perthshire's unemployment was well below the average. Differences between areas and towns in close proximity were often quite large. Chelmsford in the prosperous county of Essex had a rate of 1.6 per cent in 1937 against Pitsea's 36.4 per cent; Stafford and Kidsgrove had rates of 3.4 and 44.5 per cent respectively in the same year, while in Barnsley and Halifax the respective rates were 24.3 and 6.0 per cent.

One indication of the increasing gravity of the problem was the rise in juvenile and long-term unemployment. By 1936 roughly one-quarter of the applicants for unemployment benefit had been out of work for more than a year as against less than five per cent in 1929. In some areas the proportion was much higher and there was little tendency for it to decline during the course of the recovery in the 1930s. Juvenile unemployment rose sharply in the depression of the early 1930s, from over three per cent among boys in 1929 to 8.3 per cent in 1932, with even larger increases in the North-east, Scotland and Wales.

It is not difficult to find reasons why unemployment was so acute and persistent in this period. One was the downturn in demand, both home and export, in the sharp cyclical depressions of 1921–22, 1929–32 and 1937–38, which account for the very high levels of unemployment in these years. But throughout the period there was a hard core of unemployment of between 1–1½ million which was caused by the process of structural change taking place at this time. The big staple trades of the nineteenth century, mining, textiles, shipbuilding and mechanical engineering, suffered sharp and permanent contractions in demand for their products, especially from overseas. They were also relatively inefficient, overmanned industries and when conditions became difficult they shed labour rapidly. Thus in the first half of the 1920s employment in mining, mechanical engineering, shipbuilding, iron and steel and textiles fell by more than one million. These five large groups accounted for around one-half of the insured unemployed in July 1929, 517,496 out of a total of 1.14 million, and a similar proportion in the later 1930s.

Given the strong geographic concentration of the staple trades in the North it is easy to see why this part of the country suffered so much more than the South. Scotland, for example, was particularly vulnerable from the point of view of industrial structure. The staple industries accounted for 43.2 and 36.8 per cent of total net industrial output in 1924 and 1936 as against 37.0 and 27.8 per cent respectively for the UK as a whole; Scotland's share of the new growth industries (vehicles, electrical engineering, rayon, non-ferrous metals, paper, printing and publishing) was 8.3 and 11.0 per cent in these years, compared with national averages of 14.1 and 21.0 per cent. Scotland's problem stemmed primarily from the dramatic collapse of export demand for her once staple products. The volume of exports through Scottish ports fell by no less than 56 per cent between 1913 and 1933, and even at the peak of the recovery they were still 42 per cent below the prewar level. Heavy concentration on declining basic sectors resulted in lower productivity and a lower income per head than the rest of the country and this in turn discouraged the development of new and expanding sectors.

A similar pattern of events was repeated in other northern regions, where in some cases the old staples accounted for 60–70 per cent of the insured labour force. In the South, with its more favourable locational advantages, the pressure was eased by the rapid growth of newer industries and service trades, though even here the growth of employment was insufficient to cope with both local unemployment and the drift of workers from the North. Moreover, the problem was compounded during the period not only by the general rise in productive efficiency due to technical change, especially in manufacturing, which cut down the need for additional labour, but also by the fact that some of the new sectors of activity were more capital intensive than the old staples.

Apart from the structural and cyclical factors discussed above, two more generalised explanations need to be considered, namely government policy and real wages and welfare benefits. The first of these is mainly relevant to the 1920s when the government's resolute attempts to defend the currency and maintain the gold standard resulted in an overvalued exchange rate and relatively high interest rates. Thus general policy was not particularly conducive to rapid growth, though it is unlikely that an easier policy would have done much to alleviate the problems of the staple industries. During the 1930s policy became more favourable with devaluation and cheap money, though lacking any specific attempt to boost employment (see below).

The second factor, that of the real wage level and welfare benefits, is a more controversial issue and has recently been given a new prominence by Benjamin and Kochin (1978, 1979).[1] The crux of the issue is that employment was

---

1. D.K. Benjamin and L.A. Kochin, 'Unemployment and the Dole: Evidence from Interwar Britain', in H.G. Grubel and

lower than it would otherwise have been because of excessive wage costs; the price of labour in real terms was too high as a result of falling prices and sticky money wages due to union resistance to wage reductions. In turn the high rate of unemployment benefit impeded the drive to bring down money wages so that the unemployed of the later 1920s and later 1930s 'were pulled into unemployment, not pushed out of employment'. The authors estimate that the unemployment rate would have averaged more than a third lower had the dole been no more generous than when it was set up in 1913. In that year the benefit to wage ratio was 0.27, as against an average of 0.47 for the interwar years as a whole, with a peak of 0.6.

The argument is suggestive and in essence it is an extension of contemporary economic thinking. While there is no doubt that levels of interwar benefit were generous compared with 1913 and the early years after the Second World War, and that unemployment benefits rose substantially in real terms during the period, it is difficult to determine whether a substantial lowering of the prevailing benefit–wage ratio would have had a dramatic effect on employment. It is true that there is sporadic evidence of unemployment through 'scrounging', etc. and the enticement to remain idle when benefits were very generous, as in the case of Poplar, but the main thrust of the argument hinges on the extent to which money wages and hence real wages would have fallen had benefits been reduced, and whether this would have generated a greater demand for labour. It is difficult to conceive, for example, that it would have done much to staunch the outflow of labour from the old staple industries whose demand structure was such as to be impervious to domestic action. And if in fact a lowering of the real wage rate had effectively raised the demand for labour in the staple industries, this would have slowed down the pace of structural change.

Unemployment, whatever its causes, was undoubtedly a matter for public concern during the interwar period, yet

M.A. Walker (eds), *Unemployment Insurance: Global Evidence of its Effects on Unemployment* (Vancouver, 1978) and 'Searching for an Explanation of Unemployment in Interwar Britain', *Journal of Political Economy*, (1979).

Public work for the unemployed in January 1921. Some sporadic attempts were made at engaging the unemployed on public works, such as clearing land, making allotments, growing vegetables and building roads.

very little was done to alleviate the problem. There were of course several partial attempts to ease the situation, for example industrial transfer schemes and assisted emigration in the 1920s, reconstruction schemes and special areas legislation in the 1930s, and sporadic public works and the like, but these amounted to very little in terms of the national problem. At best they created work for a very small proportion of the unemployed, so that total unemployment would not have been very much higher had they not existed. More broadly, macroeconomic policy was not designed for purposes of work creation. During the 1920s monetary and fiscal policy were geared to protecting the currency, while in the following decade monetary policy was relaxed but fiscal restraint continued, with the additional, but dubious bonus, of tariff protection.

In the debates on this issue much attention has been devoted to explaining why macro-policy was so restrictive, or in other words, why no effort was made to produce a sharp counter-cyclical thrust to generate employment. The opportunity for a large fiscal expenditure boost was more apparent in the 1930s when the monetary constraint was relaxed with the abandonment of gold and devaluation of the pound which paved the way for cheap money. Fiscal policy however continued to be constrained by conventional economic thinking which dictated that public expenditure should be pruned and the budget balanced. Deficit financing was never seriously contemplated partly because it would have eroded confidence and partly because the orthodox Treasury view inspired the belief that it would be a wasted effort. Moreover, both the government and the trade unions were more concerned to contain the unemployment problem by subsidising the unemployed rather than subsidising jobs.

If the lack of firm policy action is readily explainable, the more intriguing question is whether there could have been a feasible solution to unemployment in the circumstances of the time. It is correct to assert that for much of the period monetary and fiscal policies were inappropriate, but it is debatable whether there was a viable alternative policy which could have solved Britain's difficulties, given the legacy of the past industrial structure and external developments over which this country had little control. For example, it is doubtful, given the changing pattern of external demand, whether easier monetary conditions and a lower exchange rate in the 1920s would have done much to alleviate the staple industries, and if they had done so whether the process of structural change would have been retarded. Certainly there was no marked change in their fortunes after 1931–32 when devaluation and cheap money came into being. The main impact of cheap money was on housebuilding and even in this case there were several other factors responsible for the housing boom of the early 1930s.

The main alternative policy strategy would have been a large expenditure boost by the government. There were however limitations to this approach apart from the obvious constraint imparted by the conventional wisdom. Glynn and Howells (1980) have calculated that to produce 2.8 million man years of employment would have required an increase of £537 million in government spending. This was equivalent to nearly 14 per cent of Gross National Product in 1932 and over 49 per cent of total public authority spending, while on the basis of the balanced budget of that year it would have involved a rise in spending or a reduction in revenue (through lower taxes) of some 70 per cent. As the authors remark: 'Even before one asks where the funds to meet the deficit might have come from, the required amount can already be seen to be in the realms of political and economic fantasy.'

The implications of such a massive spending programme would have been formidable. At a time when business confidence was at a low ebb, any departure from sound finance would, given prevailing economic thinking, have caused panic and a flight of capital from the country. One has only to recall the way in which the prospect of a very much smaller budget deficit in 1931 gave rise to a major crisis of confidence. At the same time the process of financing a deficit of the magnitude required would have had deflationary implications from the monetary side, since it would have been necessary to engineer a rise in interest rates to make the issue of large amounts of government stock attractive. The alternative of printing money was a non-starter given the inflationary implications and the collapse of confidence which would have ensued. Furthermore, the leakage effects of increased spending through imports would eventually have set a balance of payments constraint to the policy.

Financial considerations apart, it is debatable whether a large fiscal boost would have provided a satisfactory or viable solution to the unemployment problem. McKibbin (1975)[2] has pointed out that the structural problems of the economy required large-scale shifts in investment patterns and the way in which the government could enforce such shifts at the time is questionable. A generalised consumer-orientated fiscal thrust would have led to overheating in the relatively prosperous regions of the South, with only a marginal impact on the depressed northern regions. A discriminatory regional policy could have been attractive provided it had induced new growth industries to locate in the North, though attempts to achieve this in the special areas were not crowned with great success since most firms were reluctant to invest in areas considered to have poor accessibility, high local taxes, low consumer purchasing power and strong and militant unions. Thus as Miller (1976)[3] argues, the only way of reviving the depressed areas was an effective state-directed employment policy, but this was scarcely a viable alternative at the time, given the National Government's commitment to private enterprise.

This still leaves the question as to the type of employment generation required. Any quick solution to the problem would have involved the creation of employment opportunities in the staple industries or in public activities, neither of which were expedient in terms of structural change and long-term growth. The alternative — the

---

2. R. McKibbin, 'The Economic Policy of the Second Labour Government 1929–1931', *Past and Present*, 58 (1975).
3. F.M. Miller, 'The Unemployment Policy of the National Government 1931–1936', *Historical Journal*, 19 (1976).

promotion of growth industries and the retraining of labour — was a slower but more viable one, both as regards structural change and the future growth of the economy.

In essence therefore, there was not then, anymore than there is today, a ready solution to the unemployment problem. The financial implications of a large Keynesian pump-priming programme limited the range of government action in a free market economy, while in the real world the type of employment generation required to soak up quickly a large pool of labour would tend to slow down the pace of structural change and weaken the long-term viability of the economy. Structural adaptation was clearly the solution to the interwar problem, but the process inevitably takes time to complete and it cannot be forced artificially by governments bent on curing unemployment. As it happens interwar governments concentrated their attention on containing the social repercussions of unemployment by subsidising the jobless, rather than creating jobs by subsidising employment. They may well have erred too far in one direction, but at least this passive policy assisted rather than retarded the process of structural change.

Study Questions on Unemployment and Economic Policy

(a) Why was unemployment so unevenly distributed among the regions of the country?

(b) Was the unemployment problem of the interwar period a structural rather than a cyclical one?

(c) Was there a feasible solution to the interwar unemployment problem?

Recommended Reading on Unemployment and Economic Policy

Benjamin, D.K. and Kochin, L.A., 'Searching for an Explanation of Unemployment in Interwar Britain', *Journal of Political Economy*, (1979).

Constantine, S., *Unemployment in Britain between the Wars* (London, 1980).

Glynn, S and Howells, P.G.S., 'Unemployment in the 1930s: The Keynesian Solution Reconsidered', *Australian Economic History Review*, 20 (1980).
Howson, S., 'Slump and Unemployment', in R. Floud and D. McCloskey, (eds), *The Economic History of Britain since 1700*, Vol. 2, *1860 to the 1970s* (Cambridge, 1981).

The Interwar Years in Retrospect

The interwar years provide a fascinating period for study, not least because of the sharp contrasts that emerge between the growing sectors of the economy and the declining industries, the prosperous regions and the depressed areas, and the high unemployment and poverty alongside expanding real incomes for the majority of the population and improved social and welfare conditions. But apart from its intrinsic interest it also has considerable relevance for some of the problems facing society today, in particular unemployment and structural change.

Though the inflationary experience of today provides a sharp contrast with the compressed price situation in the interwar years, the unemployment and structural problems of contemporary society are not without parallel with those of the 1930s. In both cases significant new technological systems were and are being grafted on to the old and, given the inevitable lumpiness of their thrust, the impact is uneven over time, and between regions and sectors of the economy. In the ensuing process of structural change the unemployment problem is pronounced, since the fall-out of labour from the older system cannot readily be absorbed because of mobility and training bottlenecks and the lower unit labour requirements of new technologies, while the inevitable lag in the learning process in identifying new consumer wants and needs produces a hiatus in the rate of investment.

In this type of situation it is difficult to formulate a viable policy which will mop up unemployment quickly. Given the scale of unemployment, together with its geographic and occupational diversity both in the 1930s and today, the stimulus required to generate the requisite employment is too large in terms of the known financial constraints, while a large expansionary boost through fiscal policy would probably do little, and may even retard, the rate of structural change and the shift to a new technological base. Indeed, the danger is that governments, faced with severe unemployment, will tend to act defensively by preserving or propping up those parts of the system which have gone ex-growth and which should be pruned, while neglecting to encourage the development of new technologies and the retraining of redundant labour with new skills. In both periods there are examples of such reactions — witness the industrial reconstruction schemes of the 1930s and the current attempts to prop up inefficient and outdated technological systems with subsidies. However, neither in the 1930s nor as yet today has a large fiscal boost been imparted, though for reasons other than that of not impeding the necessary process of technological and structural transformation.

In effect, what this means is that given the known constraints and the lumpy nature of major technological changes, there is no readily available solution to the attendant unemployment problem. It may be possible to provide temporary alleviation, but modern theory, no less than classical theory, cannot provide a short-cut answer to the problem at a time of major technological and structural transformation.

General Reading List

Aldcroft, D.H., *The Interwar Economy: Britain, 1919–1939* (London, 1970)

Alford, B.W.E., *Depression and Recovery? British Economic Growth 1918–1939* (London, 1972)

Floud, R. and McCloskey, D., *The Economic History of Britain since 1700*, Vol. 2, *1860 to the 1970s* (Cambridge, 1981)

Kahn, A.E., *Great Britain in the World Economy* (New York, 1946)

Kirby, M.W., *The Decline of British Economic Power since 1870* (London, 1981)

Lewis, W.A., *Economic Survey, 1919–1939* (London, 1949)

Pollard, S., *The Development of the British Economy, 1914–1950* (London, 1962)

Sayers, R.S., *A History of Economic Change in England, 1880–1939* (London, 1967)

Williams, L.J., *Britain and the World Economy, 1919–1970* (London, 1971)

Youngson, A.J., *Britain's Economic Growth, 1920–1966* (London, 1967)

Index

Agricultural Credits Acts (1923, 1928), 37, 85
Agricultural Marketing Acts (1931, 1933), 38
agriculture, 29–34, 36–40
 decline in, 38
 effect of war on, 36, 39–40
 employment in, 38
 government aid to, 37–8, 39
 marketing legislation, 38
 migration from, 38
 production structure, 37, 38–9, 40
 productivity in, 39
 rate relief, 38
archery, 126

balance of payments, 79–81
 capital account, 80–81
 current account, 80, 81
 deterioration in, 79–81
 invisibles, 80, 81
 overseas lending, 80, 81
 summary date, 81
 trade deficit, 80, 81

balance of trade, 80, 81
Balfour Committee (1926–30), 35
Bank of England, 87, 88, 91, 92, 93
 policy, 91–2, 94
Bank Rate, 91, 92, 93, 94, 95, 96
banks, 83, 84, 85, 86
 commercial bills, holdings of, 88
 policy of, 87, 88
 Treasury bills, holdings of, 88
Barnsley, 134
Belgium, 93, 95
betting, 124
Bevin, Ernest, 120
birth-rate, 23
 factors causing decline in, 23
births, 21, 22, 23
Blackpool, 128
boom (1919–20), 5, 12–13, 49
 (1930s), 19
Boots Pure Drug Company, 68, 123
bowls, 126
boxing, 126, 127

147

British Airways, 62
British Broadcasting Corporation (1926), 53, 124
British Home Stores, 68
British Overseas Airways Corporation (1939), 53, 62
British Sugar Corporation, 38
British Sugar Subsidy Act (1925), 38
British Trade Corporation, 84
building and construction industry, 16, 30, 31, 32, 33, 34, 42 *passim*
building materials, 43 *passim*
building societies, 83, 84, 85
Burton, 123
bus and coaches (*see under* road transport)

Cable Makers' Association, 55
Canada, 8, 9
canals, 58
capital stock, 30, 31, 32, 33–4, 43 *passim*
Census of Production (1935), 53, 54
Central Electricity Board (1926), 53
Chelmsford, 134
chemical industry, 30, 53
cinema, 124, 125
  attendances, 126
civil aviation, 58
  domestic, 63
  imperial routes, 62
  overseas, 62
  unprofitability of, 62–3
clothing, 43
coal industry, exports of, 73
  (*see also under* mining)
commercial bills, 83, 88
consumer durables, 122
consumers' expenditure, 5, 6, 7, 13, 18
  distribution of, 121–2
  on transport, 58, 60
co-operative societies, 67
Corn Production Acts (1917, 1920), 36, 37

Cornwall, 134
County War Agricultural Committees, 40
Crook, 129, 131
Cunliffe Committee (1918), 84, 91
currency, 90, 91
  policy on, 92–3, 94–6
currency and credit, 90–97
  (*see also under* financial policy; gold standard; monetary policy; and sterling)
cycling, 127, 128

dancing, 126
death rate, 24
  causes of fall in, 24
deaths, 23
Denmark, 8, 9
departmental stores, 67–8
depression, 5, 8
  (1921), 13
  (1930s), 16–7, 45
  recovery from, 18–9
devaluation, 17, 18, 75, 136, 139, 140
Devon, 134
discount companies, 83, 84
distributive trades, 31, 32, 33, 34, 64–71
  employment in, 66
  (*see also under* retailing; and wholesaling)
domestic living conditions, 122–3
domestic service, 30, 33, 127
drink, 30, 43 *passim*
  decline in consumption of, 122, 123

earnings, 107, 108
  fluctuations in, 109–10
  real 108, 111, 119
  rise in, 111
economic growth, 1, 4–11, 15
  comparative, 7–11
  and factor inputs, 31–4, 42 *passim*
  recovery in (early 1920s), 13, 15, 49
  (1930s), 5–6, 18, 19

INDEX

economic policy (*see under* fiscal policy; industrial policy; and monetary policy)
education, 15
Education Act (1918), 115
electrical engineering, 16, 19, 43 *passim*
electricity, 15, 30, 31, 32, 33, 34, 42, 43 *passim*, 104, 105, 122
employment, 13, 17, 19
  distribution of, 66
  in entertainment and sport, 124
  growth of, 30–4, 108
  index of, 108
  loss of, in staple industries, 135
  by sector, 31–4
  subsidisation of, 142
engineering, 30, 43 *passim*, 135
English Journey, 127
entertainment, 124–8
Essex, 134
Exchange Equalisation Account, 95
exports, 5, 6, 7, 9, 10, 13, 15, 16, 18, 19, 63, 79, 80
  coal, 73, 74
  composition of, 74
  decline of, 72, 73
    reasons for, 73–5
  import substitution, 74
  indices of, 73
  invisible exports, 80, 81
  loss of competitiveness, 75
  as proportion of national income, 72
  Scottish decline in, 135–6;
  share of world exports, 74
  structure of exports, 74
  in wartime, 77

factor inputs, 31–3, 43 *passim*
family size, 23, 121
Far East, 16
Farrington Committee (1916), 85
ferrous metals, 19
financial institutions, 83–8
  commercial bills, decline of, 88
  and government policy, 85, 87
  growth of assets, 83–4
  Treasury bills, 88
financial policy, 84, 85, 87, 88, 91 *passim*
  (*see also under* monetary policy)
First World War, 4, 5, 12, 58, 119–20
  casualties, 21
  effect of, 4–5, 12, 36–7, 98
  finance, 84, 90
  population impact, 21–2
fiscal policy, 13, 99, 101, 102, 103
  budgetary deficits, 101, 139, 140
  budgetary policy, 139
  and capital spending, 103, 105
  constraints on, 140–41
  deflationary effects of, 101, 102, 139
  and unemployment, 139, 140
fluctuations, 11, 12–19
food, 30, 43 *passim*
  consumption of, 122
football, 126, 127
football pools, 124
Forestry Commission (1919), 53
France, 8, 9, 93
Freeman, Hardy and Willis, 68
friendly societies, 84

gambling, 124
gas, water and electricity, 30, 31, 32, 33, 34
General Strike, 15, 86, 120
Germany, 8, 9, 17, 93, 94, 110
Gloucester, 134
gold points, 90, 91
gold standard, 17, 84, 85, 136
  abandonment of 94–95, 139
  attempt to restore, 91, 92, 93
  impact of First World War on, 90
golf, 126, 127
Greenwood, Walter, 129
greyhound racing, 124, 126, 127
Gross Domestic Product, 5, 6, 7, 10, 13, 15, 19, 31
Gross National Product, 30
  distribution of, 30

Halifax, 134
Hannington, Wal, 130
Hastings, 128
health service, 114
hiking, 128
hire-purchase companies, 84, 88
holidays, 119, 127–8
  number of holidaymakers, 119, 127–8
  seaside holidays, 127–8
Holidays with Pay Act (1938), 119, 127
Home and Colonial Stores, 68
horse-drawn vehicles, 60, 127
horse-racing, 124
hours of work, 119
housebuilding, 13, 15, 16, 26, 48–9
  government aid to, 85, 87
Housing and Town Planning Act (1919), 85
hunger marches, 130

Imperial Airways, 62
Imperial Chemical Industries (ICI), 53
Import Duties Act (1932), 38
imports, 79, 80
  composition of, 76
  food, 76
  indices of, 73
  manufactures, 76, 77
  oil, 76
  raw materials, 76
  relative to GNP, 77
  rise in, 75
  in wartime, 77
India, 16, 74
industrial organisation, 51–6
  company organisation, 51–2
  concentration in, 53–6
  small firms, 55–6
  trade associations, 55–6
industrial policy, 53, 139, 145
industrial production, 5, 6, 7, 10, 13, 15, 17, 19, 31, 32, 41–50
  importance of, 41–2
  new industries, 46–50

sectoral shifts in, 42 *passim*
staple industries, 41–3, 49
insurance companies, 83, 84
investment, 13, 15, 18, 19, 48
  overseas, 80–1
  public, 99, 103, 105
  shift in investment patterns required, 141
iron and steel industry, 15, 43 *passim*
Italy, 9

joint stock companies, 52

Keynes, J.M., 93
Kidsgrove, 134
Kredit-Anstalt, 94

Land Settlement (Facilities) Act (1919), 37
Land (Utilisation) Act (1931), 37
leather, 43
leisure activities, 123–8
life expectancy, 24
Lipton, 123
Littlewoods, 68
local authorities, 53
  capital investment by, 105
  expenditure of, 99, 101
London, 27, 81, 90, 95
London Passenger Transport Board (1933), 53
Love on the Dole, 129

Macmillan Committee (1931), 85
manufacturing, 31, 32, 43 *passim*, 136
Marks and Spencer, 68, 123
means test assistance, 117
medicine, 24
merchant banks, 88
metal goods, 43
Midlands, 27, 28, 51, 134
migration, 25
  overseas, 24–5, 27, 64
  regional, 25–6, 27
  suburban, 25
mining, 30, 31, 32, 33, 34, 43 *passim*

INDEX

monetary policy, 13, 17, 91, 92, 93 *passim*, 136
  cheap money policy, 95–6, 136, 139
  impact of, 140
  and unemployment, 139
moral codes, 121, 126
motor cycles, 127
motor transport (*see under* road transport)
multiple shops, 68–70
music-halls, 126

National Government, 141
National Savings Bonds, 84, 96
Netherlands, 9, 95
new industries, 15, 18, 19, 42, 135
  importance of, 46–50
  share of net output, 135
New York, 94
  stock exchange collapse, 94
newspapers, 123, 124
non-ferrous metal manufacture, 43
Norfolk, 134
North, the, 51, 117
  economic disadvantages of, 141
  industrial structure, 135–6
  unemployment contrast with South, 134
North-east, 27, 28, 134, 135
  industrial structure, 136
North-west, 27, 134
Northern Ireland, 134
Norway, 8, 9
novels, 124

Orwell, George, 129, 131
overseas trade, 72–8, 79–80
  impediments to, 88
  (*see also under* exports; imports; and balance of payments)

paper and printing, 30
Paris, 94
pensions, 114–15
Perthshire, 134

Pitsea, 134
poor relief, 117
population, 21–7
  ageing of, 24
  change in, 22
  effect of war on, 21–2
  movements in, 25–7
Post Office, 53
  capital investment by, 105
Post Office Savings Bank, 83, 84, 87
postal services, 64
poverty, 116, 117, 118, 128
  causes of, 129
  contemporary evidence on, 129–30
  extent of, 129
  regional disparities in, 117
precision instruments, 43
prices, 13, 17, 109, 110
  retail, 108
Priestley, J.B., 127
productivity, 5, 6, 15, 19, 30 *passim*, 43 *passim*
public expenditure, 17, 51, 99, 102–3
  investment, 99, 103, 105
  reduction in, 101
  on social services, 115
  structure of, 100
  and unemployment, 138 *passim*
public finance, 98–106
  deflationary policy, 101
  (*see also under* fiscal policy)
public houses, 123
public ownership, 52–3

radio, 124
railways, 53, 58
  competition from motor transport, 61–2
  costs and charges, 61–2
  investment in, 105
  passenger miles travelled by, 60
  stagnation of, 60–2
rambling, 126
real incomes, 5, 10, 13, 17, 18, 19, 77, 119

change in, 111, 112, 117
  income per head, 112
rearmament, 19, 102–3
redistribution of incomes, 115, 116
Reith, Lord, 124
retailing, 67–71
  co-operative societies, 67
  departmental stores, 67–8
  large-scale units, 70
  multiple shops, 68, 80
  product variety, 67–70
  in wartime, 70–71
road transport, 53, 58, 60
  bus and coach travel, 60, 61, 127
  competitor to railways, 61–2
  private motoring, 58, 59, 60, 61, 127
Road to Wigan Pier, The, 129

Sainsbury, 123
salaried workers, 110–111
Scotland, 27, 134, 135
  export decline, 135–6
  industrial structure and unemployment, 135–6
seaside resorts, 127–8
Second World War, 7, 23, 39–40, 70–71, 77
  financial policy in, 96–7
  trade unions and, 120
service industries, 16, 31, 32, 33, 34
shipbuilding, 15, 19, 43 *passim*, 135
shipping, 58, 60
  conservatism of British shipowners, 64
  stagnation in, 63–4
shopping patterns, 123
  (*see also* retailing)
sliding scale wage agreements, 110
Small Holdings and Allotments Act (1926), 37
sobriety, 123
social revolution, 130

containment of, 131, 132
South, the, 51, 117, 134
  industrial structure of, 135–6
  unemployment contrast with North, 134
South Africa, 16
South America, 16, 74
South-east, 27
Southend, 128
South-west, 27
special areas, 139
speedway-racing, 126, 127
sport, 124, 126–7
  popularity of, 126–7
Stafford, 134
standard of living, 23, 24, 108 *passim*, 117, 121, 128, 131, 133
  (*see also* poverty)
staple industries, 2, 18, 41–2, 49, 51, 61, 134, 137, 140
  decline of, 135
state control of economic activity, 98–9
sterling, 90, 94, 95, 96
  management of, 95, 140
  overvaluation of, 93, 136, 140
  pegging of, 90, 91
strikes, 13, 120
structural transformation, 2, 142, 145–6
structure of economy, 29–34, 140
  industrial structure, 41 *passim*
  need for structural change, 141–2
  regional imbalance, 135–6
  regional shifts in activity, 51
suburban development, 25, 26, 123
Suffolk, 134
sugar beet industry, 38
Sweden, 2, 8, 9
swimming, 126
Switzerland, 9, 95

tariffs, 75
  effect on imports, 76–7

INDEX

taxation, 99
 and income redistribution, 116
 reductions in, 101, 102
 structure of, 100–101
taxis, 60
technical change, 42, 136, 145–6
telegraphic services, 64
telephones, 64
 number of subscribers, 64
tennis, 126, 127
terms of trade, 18
 improvement in, 80
textiles, 19, 31, 43 passim, 53, 135
theatres, 126
timber and furniture, 43 passim
Timothy White and Taylor, 68
tobacco, 30, 43 passim
trade associations, 55–6, 87
trade unions, 119–20
tramways, 58, 60
transport and communications, 19, 30, 31, 32, 33, 34, 42 passim, 58–64
Treasury, 139
Treasury bills, 83, 88, 91, 94, 96
Treasury, deposit receipts, 96
trolleybuses, 60
trustee savings banks, 83, 84

unemployment, 2, 4, 10, 13, 14 17, 18, 19, 107, 110, 117, 138, 144–5
 causes of, 135–7
 contemporary parallels, 144–5
 impact of welfare benefits on, 135–7
 juvenile, 134–5
 long-term, 134–5
 percentage rates of, 108, 133
 policy constraints, 140, 145
 policy lacking, 139
 regional incidence of, 134
 types of, 19
unemployment insurance, 114
Union Cold Storage, 68
United Dominions Trust, 85
United States, 8, 9, 13, 16, 17, 74, 93, 95, 110
USSR, 90

vehicle manufacturing, 15, 19, 42 passim, 61
 mass production techniques, 61

wages, 13, 18
 fluctuations in, 109–10
 real, 18, 107, 108, 117, 137
 rise in, 111
 wage costs and unemployment, 136
 wage rates, 108, 110, 112
Wales, 27, 28, 134, 135
Waugh, Evelyn, 129
ways and means advances, 92
welfare benefits and unemployment, 136–7
 (see also welfare policy)
welfare policy, 114 passim
 expenditure on, 115
 extension of services, 114–15
 redistribution of income through, 115, 116
 and unemployment, 136–7
Wheat Act (1932), 38
wholesaling, 66–7
Wodehouse, P.G., 129
Woolworth, F.W., 68, 69, 123

Youth Hostels Association, 128